Whin Close Warriors

A brief history of Sedgeford Aerodrome and its flying units

David Jacklin

Published by David Jacklin

2 Fairways, Stuston, Diss
Norfolk IP21 4AB

01379 741884
email: djacklin@aol.com

ISBN 978 0 9558788 0 0

Come to the edge.

We might fall.

Come to the edge.

It's too high!

COME TO THE EDGE!

And they came,

and he pushed,

and they flew.

by Christopher Logue

This booklet is dedicated to all those fledgling airmen who flew from Sedgeford aerodrome, particularly those who lost their lives in the course of their duty.

CONTENTS

Preface

Most people admire those early aviators who fought in the First World War. Aviation was in its infancy, and the flying machines were fragile and unreliable. The airmen seemed like knights of old, fighting for noble causes in a lost age of chivalry. The most successful of them, the so-called *aces*, had nicknames to personify this myth. The most famous was probably Germany's Manfred von Richthofen, known as the '*Red Baron*', who was buried with full military honours by allied soldiers in black armbands when he was finally shot down in 1918, despite the fact that he had destroyed 80 allied aircraft in air combat. His coffin was later disinterred and carried through Germany on a ceremonial train to a hero's burial in Berlin.

Flying aces like Richthofen and the allied heroes, like Mannock, Bishop and Ball, played a major role in recruiting young men to join their ranks, with the promise of action and adventure in these new flying machines. The main war zone was the Western Front, an entrenched, muddy battle line that stretched across France from the North Sea to Switzerland. The young airmen from Britain went to France with the Royal Flying Corps or the Royal Naval Air Service, being the two flying organisations that existed at that time. Sadly, like their comrades below them in the trenches, many did not survive the conflict. Moreover, air power became ever more lethal, causing death and destruction on an unprecedented scale. What began as aerial reconnaissance became very much more aggressive as the two sides bombed each other and fought for supremacy of the air.

Back in the relative calm of the home front, people were also traumatised. Every family with a soldier on the Western Front feared the dreaded telegram announcing the death or injury of a loved one who had 'gone over the top' in battle. For the first time in history, people were frightened of being bombed from the air by Zeppelin airships or Gotha bombers. To counter this new threat from the air, and to train the many airmen that were required on the Western Front and other theatres of war, several new airfields (then called aerodromes) were built throughout East Anglia. Many Norfolk towns and villages were invaded by young men and women in uniform. Military vehicles were everywhere. New fangled flying machines roared overhead terrifying the locals and their livestock. The war had reached home. Nowhere was this more evident than in the small north-west Norfolk village of Sedgeford, where, in 1915, at the beginning of World War One, an aerodrome was created east of the village, close to the road leading towards Docking and Fakenham.

Sedgeford aerodrome was initially used as a landing ground by the Royal Naval Air Service, in its efforts to counter the Zeppelin threat prevalent at that time. It was later used by the Royal Flying Corps and its successor the Royal Air Force,

mainly as a training aerodrome to prepare squadrons that were being deployed to the Western Front. As members of training squadrons, young airmen received their combat training at Sedgeford and other Norfolk aerodromes, such as nearby Narborough. For a few short years, the skies above Norfolk were alive with the sights and sounds of canvas-covered biplanes as these fledgling aviators prepared for war. To supplement their elementary flying training, the young airmen were put through an intensive programme of low-level and cross-country formation flying and gunnery practice. Many did not make it to the end of this training. Those that were deemed unsuitable were eliminated at various stages along the way, and others were unfortunately killed in flying accidents. Only the most able of these young airmen were retained in squadrons that became operational and departed for the Western Front. Some of Sedgeford's young fledglings became aces in combat, by shooting down at least five enemy aircraft. Others perished before they had achieved such distinction. All deserve to be remembered for their bravery and for the sacrifices they made.

After what seemed like an eternity of human sacrifice and slaughter, the war came to an end in November 1918, and the war-weary nation celebrated its hard won victory. Life soon returned to normal in Sedgeford, as the aerodrome closed as part of the inevitable reductions that were imposed in the post-war period. Although a few dilapidated buildings remain today, there is little to remind us of the former aerodrome and the brave young airmen who trained for war. To ensure that their story and sacrifices are not forgotten, this booklet will attempt to remember those Sedgeford-trained fledglings and their contribution to the war effort.

I gratefully acknowledge the information gleaned from the references listed at the end of the text and from the many aviation internet sites that I have accessed. I am also very grateful to the generous individuals who have helped by proofreading the text or by offering other suggestions. I am aware that this is not the complete story of Sedgeford aerodrome and its brave young airmen, and would welcome additional information to incorporate into future revisions. My contact details are included at the back of the book.

David Jacklin **December 2007**

The Language of the Air

You will meet a confusing array of aircraft names in this book. The RFC/RAF airmen of that time would refer to an aircraft, which was called an *aeroplane,* as a "*bus*", "*machine*", or a "*tub*", as the mood took them. The latter term meant a heavy, unwieldy machine. The various types of aeroplanes were generally known by their makers' names, but others were known simply as the "*Camel*", the "*Rumpty*", the "*Snipe*", the "*Pup*", the "*Dolphin*", etc. If the maker was *De Havilland*, they were generally given the "*DH*" prefix, such as a *DH4* or a *DH9*.If the aeroplane was manufactured by the Royal Aircraft Factory, which was later renamed the Royal Aircraft Establishment, they were given a two-letter prefix: *"BE"* meant *Bleriot Experimental* or *British Experimental*; *"FE"* indicated *Farman Experimental* or *Fighting Experimental*; *"RE"* meant *Reconnaissance Experimental;* and *"SE"* was for *Scouting Experimental.* Examples were *BE2C*, *FE2C*, *SE5* and *RE8*. The *RE8* was also known as the "*Harry Tate*", after a popular music hall performer of the time. Most aircraft were biplanes, but a triplane was known as a "*tripehound*". The landing ground or airfield was usually known as an *aerodrome* or just a "*drome*".

In this book every effort will be made to use this WWI vernacular, but modern terms like *aircraft* and *airfield* will inevitably creep into the text.

Origins during the Great War

The former First World War aerodrome[1] of Sedgeford was built in 1915 on the south side of the road between Sedgeford and Docking in west Norfolk. It was situated about one mile from the village of Sedgeford, around a small plantation known as ***Whin Close***, as highlighted on the following map segment.

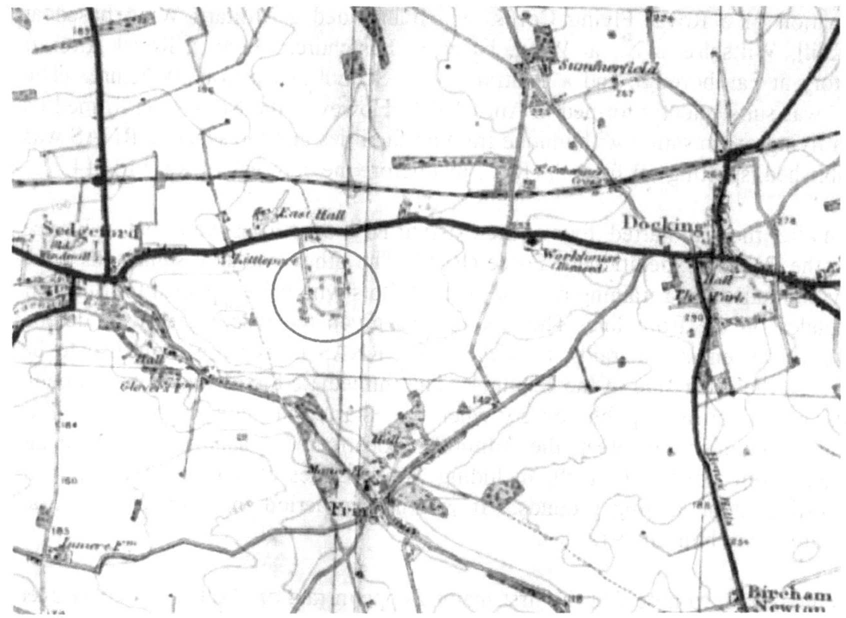

The aerodrome began life with the Royal Navy. It was first used in October 1915, as a night landing ground for the Royal Naval Air Service (RNAS) station at South Denes, Great Yarmouth. South Denes had a number of satellites, called night landing grounds, around Norfolk, including Sedgeford and nearby Narborough. These satellites were essential because of the limited range and endurance of the aircraft available at that time.

In 1916 the aerodrome was transferred to the Royal Flying Corps (RFC) and subsequently to the Royal Air Force (RAF), when the latter was created in April 1918 using the combined assets of the RFC and RNAS. To understand these changes of command it is necessary to briefly examine Britain's military aviation during that period of history.

1. Please note that *aerodromes are now called airfields* in modern terminology

Military aviation had its roots in the Army (Royal Engineers) and the Royal Navy, although their aspirations were quite different, with the Army wanting to concentrate on battlefield reconnaissance and artillery observations, while the Navy was gravely concerned about the threat from submarines and other naval matters. The concept of unified air power was born in 1911 when Prime Minister Asquith instructed the Committee of Imperial Defence to study the situation and recommend measures to rationalise things. The Committee recommended the formation of a Royal Flying Corps, which included a Military Wing based at Larkhill, Wiltshire, a Naval Wing, based at Eastchurch, Kent, a Royal Aircraft Factory at Farnborough and a Central Flying School at Upavon, Wiltshire. The RFC was subsequently formed in April 1912. However, the Navy soon formed its own flying organisation with unique training facilities and the separate RNAS was established, splitting off from the RFC, just before the outbreak of war in 1914.

Soon after the war started, four of the existing RFC squadrons were sent to France with the British Expeditionary Force (BEF). The other available squadrons were fully committed to a training role, preparing pilots who were destined to join their comrades on the front line. The RNAS was given the responsibility to defend Britain from enemy air-raids, although many RNAS units were soon also to be based on the other side of the Channel. The immediate threat was from Zeppelin raids, which caused a public outcry when they started in the early months of the war. To counter the threat, the Admiralty constructed a handful of coastal air stations from London to Hull, including South Denes at Yarmouth, with their supporting night landing grounds. It was in this period that the aerodrome at Sedgeford was built in 1915.

It is interesting to note that the first major Zeppelin raid on the UK occurred over Norfolk on the night of the 19th and 20th of January 1915, when several towns and villages were attacked causing some fatal casualties and property damage. The attack started at Great Yarmouth at about 8:30 pm, when six bombs were dropped and two individuals lost their lives. Soon afterwards the airships were seen over Cromer and Sheringham. Much later, at about 10 pm, they were sighted at Hunstanton, having been seen circling several villages, including Brancaster, where a bomb was dropped near the church. Between 10 and 11 pm, the Zeppelins were seen or heard over Dersingham, Snettisham, Sandringham, Grimston and

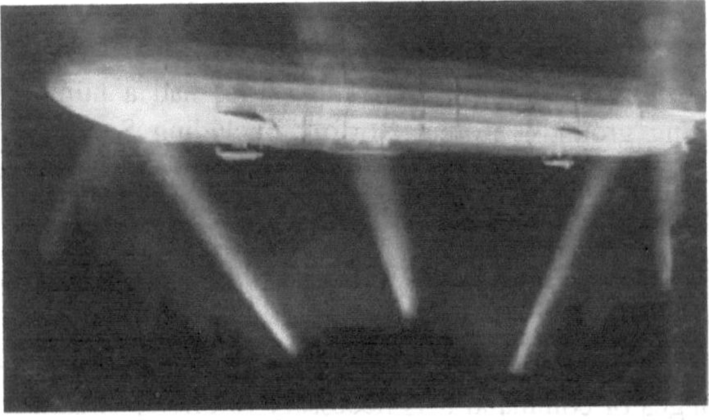

Castle Rising. Bombs were dropped on Snettisham and Heacham, but no casualties resulted from this.

This photograph shows an unexploded bomb dropped from one of the Zeppelins on Heacham, one of Sedgeford's neighbouring villages

Attempts were made to bomb the royal residence at Sandringham, but the bombs that were dropped exploded well away from Sandringham House, and the Royal Family was not in residence at the time. Finally, at about 11 pm, the Zeppelins reached King's Lynn, dropping several bombs on the town, killing two more individuals before flying out over the Wash on their homeward journey.

By June 1915, a further seventeen raids had taken place against east coast targets reaching as far south as Dover. Some of the most southern targets had been subjected to enemy aircraft attacks by Gotha bombers as well. This lead to a public outcry and resulted in changes in responsibility for home defence.

The military Wing of the RFC continued to expand during the first two years of the war in order to meet the needs of an expanding BEF. By mid 1916, RFC strength was over 420 aircraft in twenty-seven squadrons at home and abroad. These expansions included aerial reconnaissance, bombing and fighting capabilities. This had also lead to a massive increase in training facilities at home. Consequently, the War Office decided that responsibility for home defence should be transferred from the Admiralty to the RFC. As a result, Sedgeford, Narborough and other former RNAS stations were transferred to the RFC in the spring of 1916.

Sedgeford was mainly used as a training facility, preparing squadrons that were being deployed to the Western Front and other theatres of war. Like that intrepid aviator *Biggles*, created by Captain W.E. Johns, many young pilots found themselves at Norfolk aerodromes undergoing intensive flying training in preparation for war. Most of the young pilots had only completed elementary flying training and had to be toughened up in a very short period to prepare them for combat. The RFC also formed many new squadrons as home defence units. These units also required airfields from which to operate, and a major airfield construction and expansion programme was initiated throughout the east coast region. Consequently, although Sedgeford was primarily a training aerodrome, it was also used as a landing ground for squadrons involved in home defence activities. One such squadron was 51 Squadron based at nearby Marham.

In August 1917 Lloyd George appointed a Committee chaired by General Smuts to look into the future of the RFC and RNAS. As a result of this enquiry, a final rationalisation of airpower occurred by Act of Parliament at the end of November 1917, when the establishment of an Air Force and Air Council received Royal Assent. The Royal Air Force was subsequently created on the 1st of April 1918, subsuming the RFC and the RNAS. Accordingly, Sedgeford aerodrome was transferred to the RAF to complete its third change of command. Sedgeford continued as a training aerodrome under the RAF. Potential fighter pilots now had to attend Fighting Schools, which were reorganised when the RAF was formed by amalgamating the former RFC Schools of Aerial Fighting and Aerial Gunnery. By late 1918, Sedgeford became the home of No. 3 Fighting School, which will be introduced later.

The standard training units were called *reserve squadrons,* later renamed *training squadrons*. These were sub-divided into elementary flying training squadrons and higher training squadrons. These training squadrons were responsible for training pilots for active service squadrons and for creating the nucleus of new active service squadrons. With the expansion of the RFC the number of training squadrons had increased to such an extent that it was necessary to organise them into *wings,* where a wing consisted of a number of squadrons. During its tenure as a RFC aerodrome, Sedgeford trained squadrons belonging to 7 Wing. Wings, in turn, were organised in geographical groupings called *brigades* (the Southern, Northern, Eastern and Western Training Brigades). At the time when the RAF was formed, in April 1918, Sedgeford and Narborough comprised *7th Wing* of the *Eastern Training Brigade*, with a wing headquarters in King's Lynn. In addition to training squadrons, operational or *active service squadrons* arrived at Sedgeford or were formed at Sedgeford to complete 'working up' periods prior to their assignments overseas. These were not strictly training squadrons, but were active service squadrons under training, equipped with training aircraft until their front-line aircraft arrived. Accordingly, these squadrons will not be given the *reserve* or *training* prefix when they are described in the text.

Each RFC reserve, training and active squadron was allocated a squadron number. This squadron number was generally retained when a squadron was declared operational and moved to France or to another war zone. Moreover, these RFC squadron numbers were retained within the Royal Air Force when it was formed in April 1918. No. 110 Squadron RFC, for example, became No. 110 Squadron RAF while it was serving at Sedgeford. In contrast, former RNAS squadrons were renumbered by the RAF, usually by adding 200 to the original squadron number.

When the First World War started in 1914, it was little over 10 years since Orville and Wilbur Wright had left the ground on their historic first recorded flight, and a mere five years since Blériot had first crossed the English Channel. Aviation was in its infancy, and the early aeroplanes were fragile and unreliable, constructed of wood and canvas with a profusion of struts and wires. Consequently, when the RFC first went to France with the BEF, the aeroplanes were initially only used in unarmed reconnaissance roles, and were often shot at by anti-aircraft guns, known as 'Archies'. However, aviation soon became more complex. In the observation role, airborne observers not only spotted and reported on enemy movements, but also helped the army to target their artillery fire. By developing communications systems with the gunners, the aviators could help to correct the accuracy of artillery fire. This allowed for indirect targeting, where the gunners did not have to see their targets to attack them. Also, by using the eyes of the aviators, the gunners could remain hidden from the enemy. An airborne observer was able to send radio messages to tell the gunners if their rounds were falling left, right, short or beyond their intended targets, thereby improving their accuracy. However, such a system relied on air superiority. Fighter aeroplanes and tactics were developed to rid the skies of enemy observation planes, allowing one's own observers to operate with impunity. The fighter aeroplanes, called *scouts* during the First World War, were specifically designed for attacking other aircraft, as opposed to bomber aeroplanes, which were designed to attack ground targets by dropping bombs. These scouts, which were generally small, fast, heavily armed, and highly manoeuvrable, were the primary means by which the RFC tried to gain this advantage. Aerial warfare became more aggressive and sophisticated as the two sides struggled for air superiority over the battlefields of the Western Front. As the war progressed, this aerial struggle raged to new levels of ferocity, as both sides fought to gain this aerial advantage. The struggle was not won by the allies until the winter of 1917-18, when they succeeded in suppressing the German air force by sheer numbers of combat aircraft. Another aspect was aerial bombardment, initially only targeting military targets, but later extended to bombing civilian centres of population. As the war progressed, air power became more and more critical to the success of most battlefield operations.

These more aggressive forms of warfare were eventually incorporated into the training at Sedgeford, which included aerial gunnery and bombing practice. The aircraft used in the training also mirrored the advances in aviation that occurred during the war years, ranging from the early 'pusher' types, with the propeller pushing the aeroplane from behind, to the latest fighters possessing synchronised machine-guns that could fire bullets through a propeller at the front of the plane. Some of the aircraft were manufactured by the Royal Aircraft Factory and others by commercial companies, such as the Aircraft Manufacturing Company (Airco), A.V. Roe & Co Ltd (Avro) and Sopwith Aviation Co. Ltd (Sopwith). For the aviation enthusiast, additional information about the aircraft types will be provided in highlighted blocks within the text and at Appendix 4. These are not essential to the main story and could be skipped over if desired.

Having looked at the origins of Sedgeford aerodrome in relation to the military organisations, challenges and threats of the day, attention will now turn to some of the flying units and aircraft that used the aerodrome. This will not be an exhaustive treatment, since some units were only at Sedgeford for a few days and others visited as cadre only at the end of hostilities, merely to disband without bringing their aircraft with them. Consequently, only those flying units that stayed for a significant period of time will be covered. Several of Sedgeford's fledgling squadrons will be introduced and two squadrons will be described in more detail.

Flying Units and Aircraft

Units that used Sedgeford as an Emergency or Night Landing Ground

Although Sedgeford's primary role was the training of squadrons that were being deployed to the Western front, it was also used as an emergency landing ground by home defence units responsible for intercepting German Zeppelins. Initially, Sedgeford was used as a night landing ground by the RNAS station at South Denes (Great Yarmouth) and later, from mid 1916 onwards, also by No. 51 Squadron RFC, which was based at Marham and at other nearby aerodromes.

RNAS South Denes, Great Yarmouth

Sedgeford aerodrome was established in 1915 as a night landing ground for the RNAS station at Great Yarmouth, flying a variety of aircraft types in a home defence role, mainly to intercept Zeppelin airships. Night landing or emergency aerodromes were required because the fighter aircraft had limited range and would often need to make emergency landings far from their home airfield at Great Yarmouth. Sometimes aircraft would be placed on standby at night landing grounds to afford greater coverage against the Zeppelin threat. Consequently, it is known that RNAS aircraft would have been in residence at Sedgeford on occasions, in addition to those that made emergency landings at the end of Zeppelin patrols. When 45 Squadron RFC arrived at Sedgeford in May 1916, to prepare for their imminent deployment to France, the RNAS presence included a flight shed which occasionally housed a BE2c night fighter. The officer responsible for this detachment was Lieutenant H.C. Mallet RN, and the pilot specifically assigned to Sedgeford at this time was Flight Sub Lieutenant J.H. Lee.

Home defences were in a poor state during those early war years. Anti-aircraft guns had little effect on Zeppelins above 10,000 feet, and the airships could soar above most fighter aircraft of the day. Consequently, the Zeppelins generally raided at high altitude and at night, and the RNAS aircraft had the almost impossible task of patrolling for airships along the coast in the dark. To overcome some of these difficulties the RNAS stationed two high-flying DH4 aircraft at Great Yarmouth. These aircraft could fly as high as the Zeppelins, but they were not seaplanes. If they were forced down over water, they would sink. It was therefore decided that they would be accompanied by an American Curtiss flying boat whenever they were over water.

For night raids, the tactics had to be altered. Instead of launching all of the aircraft at once in a haphazard search for the raiders, a system of patrols was developed. The patrols were conducted at different altitudes – say at ten, eleven and twelve thousand feet - so that aircraft would not collide with each other in the dark. Each pilot would have his allocated 'beat' and would patrol at his allocated altitude for two hours and then come down. A second pilot would then take his place to continue the search. Such relays would continue until the raiders were intercepted or the danger passed. The aircraft had to be fitted with instrument lights, so that the pilots could read their altitude, speed, engine revs and oil pressure at night. Also, to assist with night landings, the landing strips had to be illuminated by flares. These were usually two-gallon petrol cans with the tops cut off and half filled with cotton waste and soaked in paraffin.

The RNAS airmen reaped their revenge on the Zeppelins during their final raid on United Kingdom on the evening 5th of August 1918. Five Zeppelins of the German Navy had been despatched to attack targets in the Midlands, but the raid failed when they were attacked by two de Havilland DH4 aircraft from Great Yarmouth. One airship, Zeppelin L70, carrying the Chief of the German Naval Airship Division, Peter Strasser, was shot down near Wells-next-the-Sea, with no survivors and a second one was damaged. The surviving airships dropped their bombs into the sea and headed home. The aircraft credited with destroying L70, flown by Major Egbert Cadbury, made a successful landing at Sedgeford after the mission.

This photograph shows Egbert Cadbury (right) when he was a Lieutenant

To intercept the Zeppelins, Cadbury had climbed to 16,000 feet after jettisoning his reserve fuel tank and some of his bombs. As he broke through the clouds, he saw the Zeppelins above him. He banked, climbed and attacked the largest one, ripping a large hole through the fabric and igniting the escaping gas with devastating results. The fatal shots were fired by his gunner, Captain Robert Leckie, whose hands were frozen because he had forgotten to put on his gloves when they scrambled to chase the Zeppelins. After the attack on L70, Cadbury had considered chasing the other Zeppelins, but he doubted if the DH4 would have made it back to the coast had they continued the attack. As it was, thoroughly lost above solid cloud, they were lucky to find the aerodrome at Sedgeford, about 50 miles from their base at Great Yarmouth, and to touch down safely after dark in a machine that Cadbury thought was sure to crash if landed at night. Only after he landed did he discover, to his shock and horror, that two bombs he had tried to jettison to increase his climb rate during the attack, were hung up below the wings of the DH4.

This was the second Zeppelin that Leckie had shot down. As the pilot flying an American-built Curtiss H12 flying boat on a reconnaissance mission from Great Yarmouth, Flight Sub Lieutenant Leckie and his crew downed Zeppelin L22 near the island of Terchelling on the 14th of May 1917. Leckie, who later reached the rank of Air Vice-Marshal and became the Chief of the Canadian Air Staff, was awarded the Distinguished Service Cross for this feat. All four members of his Curtiss crew were also decorated[2].

Many previous Zeppelin interceptions had been less successful than that for L22 and L70. On the night of 12 August 1915, for example, three BE2c aircraft took off from Great Yarmouth in an attempt to intercept four Zeppelins. All returned after dark with engine trouble and were damaged making heavy landings. If there was ever an aeroplane unsuited for combat it must surely have been the BE2c. The pilot was slightly to the rear of the main planes (wings) and had a fair view above and below, except where the lower wing obscured the ground in the forward direction. The observer, who sat in front of the pilot, could see practically nothing, because he was wedged in the centre section, with one wing above and another below. He was also surrounded by bracing wires. He had access to a machine gun for defence purposes, but he could not fire it forward because of the propeller. Rearwards, there were struts, wires and the tail plane to obstruct his view.

[2]*When decorations are mentioned in this book, the following mnemonics will be used:*

VC – Victoria Cross	*MM – Military Medal*
MC – Military Cross	*DFC – Distinguished Flying Cross*
DSO – Distinguished Service Order	*DSC – Distinguished Service Cross*

It should also be noted that a bar could be awarded for medals issued more than once.

Other organizational factors also reduced the effectiveness of the defence against Zeppelins. For example, the pilots lived one and a half miles away from their aircraft at the RNAS station at Great Yarmouth. One pilot wrote about this situation:

"On about five successive nights now, just as we were sitting down to dinner, a Zeppelin would be reported approaching the coast somewhere on our beat. The result was a general 'hoo-doo'. All the pilots jump into cars and dash down to the sheds, closely followed by the mechanics in lorries. As our way is right along the water front, several cars and two 4-ton lorries loaded with men hurtling down to the air station frightened the whole of Yarmouth."

In 1916, the home defence system improved with some changes of responsibility. While the RNAS continued to patrol the coast, and attacked Zeppelins over the sea, the RFC took over most of the inland home defence role.

When the RAF was formed in April 1918, the landplane assets of the RNAS station were formed into flights. Later, on the 20th of August 1918, these assets were formed into RAF squadrons. 490, 557 and 558 flights became 212 Squadron RAF; 428, 429, 454 and 455 flights became 229 Squadron RAF; and 485, 486 and 534 flights became 273 Squadron RAF. These squadrons performed coastal reconnaissance duties until the end of the war.

Two Home Defence Aircraft

Designed as a single-engine bomber, the two-seat Airco DH4 was used in the home defence role by the RNAS because of its high operating ceiling and manoeuvrability, qualities that were vital for seeking and attacking Zeppelin airships. Its armament consisted of one or two forward-firing synchronised Vickers machine guns plus at least one Lewis gun installed on a mount in the observer's cockpit. It could also carry 460 lbs of bombs under the lower wings, and was considered to be one of the most successful single-engine bombers of the First World War.

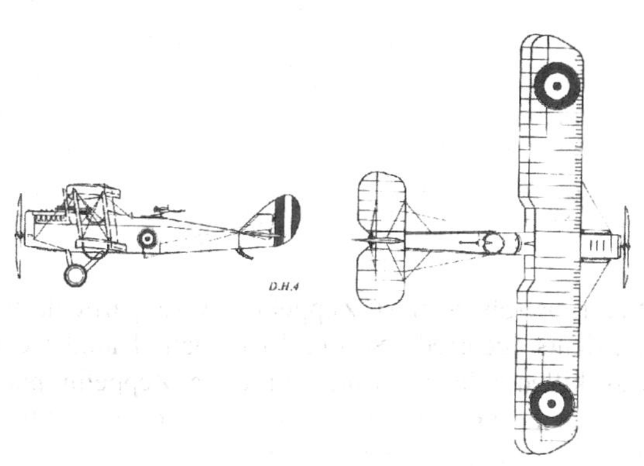

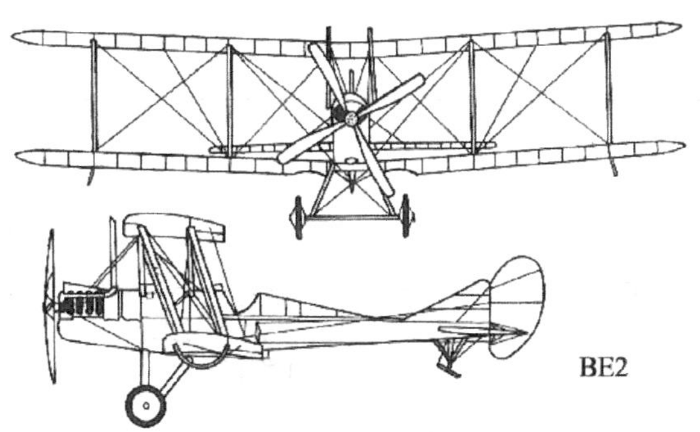
BE2

The Royal Aircraft Factory produced several versions of the two-seat BE biplanes, the most successful being the BE2c, which first appeared in 1914. This was faster and more manoeuvrable than its predecessor, the BE2a, which was considered easy prey for the more powerful and agile German aircraft. Significantly, the BE2c was better armed and could carry a larger bomb load than the BE2a, making it more suitable for the home defence role. It was also used on the Western Front by the RNAS and RFC from late 1914 until 1917. A single-seat adaptation of the BE2c, known as the BE12, was introduced with a more powerful engine. This aircraft was also used on home defence duties.

No. 51 Squadron RFC, later 51 Squadron RAF

No. 51 Squadron, RFC, was formed at Thetford on the 15th of May 1916, as a Home Defence Squadron and was originally equipped with BE2c, BE2d and BE12 aircraft. Later it received a few FE2bs. From September 1916, the squadron was established with its headquarters at Hingham and detached flights at Harling Road, Mattishall and Marham, all within easy reach of the HQ. Sedgeford was used as an emergency landing ground. In August 1917 the HQ moved to Marham, with its three flights at Marham, Mattishall and Tydd St. Mary.

Night patrols against Zeppelins were particularly dangerous and several fatal accidents occurred. Second Lieutenant Thunder crashed as he was taking off and was killed whilst setting out on a Zeppelin patrol on 23rd September 1916. Lieutenant Gaymer also crashed and was killed on the night of 27th/28th November 1916 after he had taken off in a FE2b of 51 Squadron to intercept the German airship, Zeppelin L21. However, this airship was shot down later that night by aircraft of the RNAS off Lowestoft. Six German airships raided East Anglia on the night of 24th/25th September 1917. The squadron sent two fighters from Marham, two from Mattishall and two from Tydd St Mary to intercept them, but with no success.

Avro 504K

In addition to providing protection against air attack, the Home Defence squadrons were also responsible for training pilots in night flying. At the beginning of 1918, 51 Squadron was given a special single-seat version of the Avro 504K with the forward cockpit covered over and a Lewis gun fitted above the top centre-section. This model was specially developed for night fighting, but had the added advantage of forming a suitable introductory type for the Sopwith Camel, which was also issued to 51 Squadron during 1918.

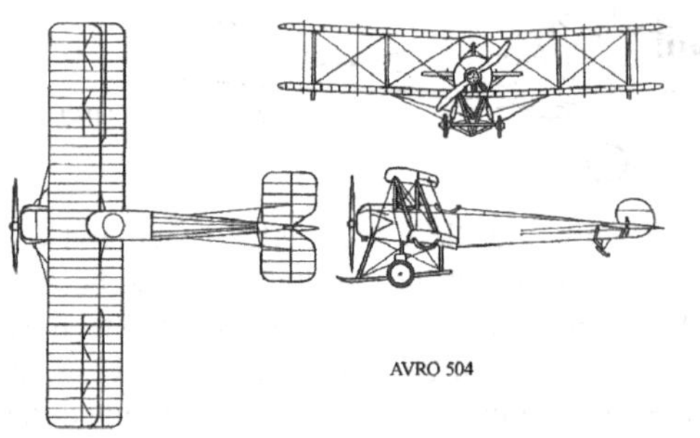
AVRO 504

One young pilot who flew with 51 Squadron for a few weeks in the autumn of 1917 was Canadian Alan Macleod, who was later to earn the Victoria Cross in France. When he first came to England he was posted to 82 Squadron flying scouts. However, when his CO found out that he was only 18, he decided that he was too young for combat, and had Alan posted to 51 Squadron. He spent two exciting weeks on Zeppelin patrols flying a BE12. He was even shot down by a Zeppelin gunner, but he managed to land his aircraft and survive. In November 1917 he was sent to the Pilot Pool at St. Omer to begin his very distinguished service in France, which resulted in him being awarded the VC for his bravery in action. This occurred when he was flying with No. 2 Squadron. He was attacked by several enemy triplanes and, despite being injured with his plane on fire, he and his observer managed to shoot down three of them. He then crash-landed in "no man's land" and pulled his injured observer from the wreckage to safety before they were rescued.

By late 1918 the HQ and 'C' Flight of 51 Squadron were still based at Marham. 'A' Flight was at Mattishall with Avro 504s, while 'B' Flight was at Tydd St Mary with FE2bs. The squadron still had Sedgeford under its control as a landing ground, along with several other aerodromes. The HQ and 'C' Flight remained at Marham until May 1919, when it left for Sutton's Farm and disbanded in June of the same year.

Units that Trained at Sedgeford

Sedgeford aerodrome was extensively used to prepare units that were to be deployed to the Western Front and other war zones. These units would arrive, or would be created locally, as training or active service squadrons, and would undergo several months of intensive flying training and gunnery practice before they achieved operational status and were transferred overseas. The training of these fledgling squadrons will be introduced in this section, together with details of their subsequent combat experience.

No. 45 Squadron RFC, later 45 Squadron RAF

No. 45 Squadron was the first Royal Flying Corps unit to use Sedgeford, arriving on the 12th of May 1916, under the command of Major William Ronald Read M.C. The Squadron flew in from Thetford with BE2c training aircraft to work up for its imminent posting to France.

Major W.R. Read

Once the squadron had settled in at Sedgeford, it was incorporated into the anti-Zeppelin defences, with one aeroplane on stand-by and the Wireless Section maintaining a listening watch to intercept Zeppelin signals traffic. The aeroplane was actually scrambled once to intercept a Zeppelin which was reported to have been sighted over Sandringham. Major Read clambered aboard to begin a pursuit, but the engine wouldn't start and the sighting was never confirmed. Zeppelins aside, the Squadron's main task at Sedgeford was to function as an advanced flying training squadron to prepare its airmen for combat in France. Much of the following information about 45 Squadron was obtained from a paper prepared by Jeff Jefford, which was subsequently published in the Cross & Cockade International Journal, Volume 30 Number 4.

A typical trainee pilot arriving at Sedgeford would have spent a few weeks at Reading or Oxford on a ground-based indoctrination course followed by some limited practical flying training at a reserve squadron. Consequently, he might have logged a dismal total of perhaps twelve hours in the air before starting his advanced training at Sedgeford. 45 Squadron required about ten aeroplanes to support its training activities, and these were provided from a large variety of different aircraft types that the squadron was able to acquire, including the BE2c type and many others. The trainee population was also continuously changing, as students graduated and others took their places.

Jefford described the training regime as 'the blind leading the blind', with only rudimentary instructional techniques, and newly qualified pilots having to pass on their limited skills to less experienced flyers. From a trainee's perspective, the training consisted of passing a written and practical examination and flying as many solo trips as possible, learning from his own mistakes. Training was essentially practice that required a dash of good luck. Several flying accidents occurred, but only two of 45 Squadron's trainees appear to have been seriously injured. Second Lieutenant James Ferme spun and crashed his BE training aeroplane on the 16th of June. He limped away, but was so badly injured that he was unable to fly again. The second casualty was Second Lieutenant Gladstone Main, who crashed another BE on the 20th of July. Like Ferme, Main survived the accident but failed to qualify for his 'wings'.

One of 45 Squadron's pilots, Captain Eric Fox Pitt Lubbock, son of Lord Avebury, will serve to illustrate the point about novice instructors. Although he had logged an impressive 28 hours solo by the time he was awarded his 'wings' at Sedgeford, he was still a novice. Despite his limited experience, he was nevertheless employed as an instructor and sent his first pupil on a solo flight on the day that he officially received his own certification. He was later seconded from 45 Squadron as part of the nucleus which formed the successor squadron at Sedgeford (No. 64 Squadron). However, after a short period with this new squadron, he returned to the fold and was appointed as the commander of 'B' Flight, proceeding to France with 45 Squadron. Tragically, Lubbock later met his death in a Strutter over the Western Front. He and his observer, Thompson, were killed over the Ypres Salient as they were returning from a photographic mission on March 11, 1917, when their Sopwith 1½ Strutter broke up in flight during combat with enemy fighters. A colleague in France, fellow pilot Norman Macmillan, who wrote an excellent book about 45 Squadron's war, '*Into the Blue*', believed that Lubbock was an unsung hero and the first outstanding fighter pilot of 45 Squadron, who had seen more combat, taken more reconnaissance photographs, and shown greater keenness than any other pilot in the Squadron.

By mid July 1916, the squadron was allocated twelve observers, but they were to spend little time at Sedgeford. Before being posted to the squadron, these observers had also undergone indoctrination courses at Reading or Oxford. When they reported to Sedgeford, most of them were given a trip in an aeroplane before being sent to Hythe to study the theory and practice of aerial gunnery. From Hythe they went on to Brooklands to spend three weeks at the Wireless School, eventually rejoining the squadron at Sedgeford prior to its move to France.

New qualification tests were introduced in March of 1916 to raise the standard of pilot training. Amongst other skills, a pilot was supposed to have flown at least 15 hours solo, have climbed to 6,000 feet and stayed there for at least 15 minutes, flown a *service* as distinct from a *training* aeroplane, made a cross-country flight of at least sixty miles (making two landings at RFC airfields on route), and have made two night landings assisted by flares. In addition, before proceeding overseas, a pilot should have had as much practice as possible in landing, bombing, aerial fighting, night flying, and formation flying. Significantly there was no requirement for combat manoeuvring, although pilots were encouraged to indulge in such activities, if time permitted, which it rarely did. Essentially, a pilot was considered to be ready for active service if he could take off, keep the aeroplane in the air and land again, with or without power!

The training at Sedgeford also included wireless telegraphy. Two of the training aircraft were fitted with radio transmitters and a receiver station was maintained on the ground. It was previously mentioned that this receiver station was also used to listen out for Zeppelin signals traffic as part of the anti-Zeppelin defences. Trainees were also required to become familiar with the artillery codes used to assist army gunners to target their artillery fire on the battlefield. A ground-based artillery target was used, which was fitted with light bulbs to simulate artillery fire. Students would transmit practice artillery messages from the aircraft in Morse code, which were picked up by the receiving station. Sadly, this training focus on artillery co-operation and wireless procedures was not relevant to the squadron's future role of photographic reconnaissance, and it did not adequately prepare it for the upcoming combat experience. Essential training on aerial gunnery and air combat tactics, so vital for survival, was not provided. These omissions would have tragic consequences, which are reflected in the squadron's abnormally high casualty figures.

Jefford provided details of 45 Squadrons initial operational establishment of officers and NCO aircrew, which is provided at Appendix 1. Many of these officers are shown on the following photograph taken at Sedgeford shortly before the squadron moved to France. Major W. R. Read commanded a squadron of eighteen aeroplanes divided into three flights. Captain G. Mountford commanded 'A' Flight; Captain E.F.P. Lubbock commanded 'B' Flight; and Captain L. Porter commanded ‘C’ Flight. In addition to the pilots and observers, there were three ground staff officers, comprising a Recording Officer and two Equipment Officers, who looked after the technical equipment, such as the vehicles and radio equipment.

As part of its mobilisation, 45 Squadron provided the nucleus of 64 Squadron, which was to succeed it at Sedgeford. An initial package of several training aircraft, surplus trainees and two experienced pilots was provided. As was previously mentioned, one of the seconded pilots was Captain The Honourable Eric Lubbock, who later returned to 45 Squadron.

45 Squadron officers photographed at Sedgeford before going to France

45 Squadron was earmarked to become a fighter-reconnaissance squadron, and it received its operational equipment, Sopwith 1½ Strutters, during the period July to September 1916 and left for France during early October. A 49-vehicle motor transport column left Sedgeford on the 4th of October, sailing from Avonmouth and Southampton on schedule. However, the movement of the air echelon was a shambles, taking almost a week to get all of the aeroplanes across the channel to the St Omer Depot and onwards to their airfield at Fienvilliers. Bad weather and technical problems caused most of the delays.

The worst was to come. Within one week of its arrival in France the squadron had six men killed in action and two more were in hospital as a result of flying accidents. There were many root causes for these high casualties. The squadron was certainly not given sufficient time to acclimatise to the Western Front before it was committed to combat, and it was also woefully ill-prepared for combat. In their training, the pilots had done very little formation flying and had little or no experience of aerial combat and air gunnery. Although the observers had been taught aerial gunnery at Hythe, most of the pilots had not. Many of the pilots were also having trouble getting used to the Sopwith Strutters, having had too little time flying this type at Sedgeford before proceeding to France. Also, as was previously mentioned, the training at Sedgeford had concentrated on artillery co-operation procedures and wireless telegraphy rather than aerial gunnery and air-combat tactics, so crucial to survival in France. Indeed, the squadron did not receive its machine guns and synchronisation gear until September 1916, only about three weeks before it was due to go to France. Improved training would be introduced from 1917 onwards to overcome many of these deficiencies, but it would arrive much too late to help 45 Squadron.

45 Squadron was in the 11th (Army) Wing of the 2nd Brigade RFC, commanded by Brigadier-General Webb-Bowen. From December 1916 until November 1917 they operated from the aerodrome of St. Marie Cappel, near the little Flemish town of Cassel (see Appendix 4). During the Somme offensive the squadron was employed on photographic reconnaissance and patrols along the Ypres Salient, where they suffered very heavy casualties. In fact the casualties were so heavy that, in April 1917, the Sopwiths were supplemented by some Nieuport two-seaters to keep the squadron going. From late October 1916 until early May 1917, 45 Squadron only achieved three confirmed kills, although two more were claimed but not confirmed. In this period 23 pilots and observers were killed and five wounded in action. In addition three were accidentally killed and one injured. Moreover, heavier casualties were to come. The Strutters were outclassed almost from the start, and it wasn't until mid-1917, when Camels arrived, that losses decreased to an acceptable level and 45 Squadron became much more successful.

Sopwith Camels of No. 45 Squadron RFC

The detailed statistics during the disastrous period flying Strutters are summarized here: 45 Squadron operated the Sopwith 1½ Strutters in France for 46 weeks. During that period it claimed 84 victories, 28 of them being 'kills'. This was quite impressive considering that the Strutters were outclassed from early 1917. The price it paid for this success was 60 combat fatalities, 4 fatalities resulting from a mid-air collision, 19 wounded and 6 more taken prisoner.

The Squadron's Commanding Officer, Major Read, who did not get on with his superiors at Wing and Brigade level, particularly his Wing commander, Lieutenant Colonel 'Stuffy' Dowding, and the Brigade commander Brigadier-General Webb-Bowen, decided to leave the RFC and return to his regiment, the King's Dragoon Guards. He departed on the 24th of April and Major H.A. Van Ryneveld MC, a South African officer, took over the reigns. Van Ryneveld was subsequently injured in combat on the 18th of August and invalided home. Command of 45 Squadron then passed to Major Vancour on the 22nd of August 1917. Read was to return to flying later in the war, first as a flying instructor and later, in 1918, to command 216 Squadron, which was part of Trenchard's Independent Force.

There were few confirmed victories during the time that Major Read commanded 45 Squadron, and no decorations were awarded. The first Military Cross was awarded to observer, Lieutenant D.C. Eglington, when he successfully flew a Strutter back to the British lines on the 20th of May 1917, after his pilot, Captain C.H. Jenkins was seriously wounded on a patrol. He achieved this feat by clinging on to the outside of the fuselage with one hand while manipulating the injured pilot's joystick with the other. Unfortunately Jenkins died three days later.

The first Squadron pilot to be decorated with the Military Cross, in June 1917, was Lieutenant (later Captain) James Dacres Belgrave, who joined the Squadron at the end of November 1916 and went on to score 6 victories flying Sopwith Strutters. After a rest spell in England he joined 60 Squadron and was credited with many more victories flying SE5s. He was killed in action on the 13th of June 1918.

By early June 1917, most of the original pilots and observers who had left Sedgeford had become casualties of war or had been taken prisoner. Only two original pilots and one observer remained. Two of them, Captain Mountford, the original commander of A Flight, and his observer, 2/Lt Vessey, were killed on the 12th of June. They had been to No. 1 Aircraft Depot at St Omer and were flying back to St Marie Cappel airfield when they collided with a Strutter, which had just taken off for a reconnaissance mission. The pilot of the other aircraft, Watt, and his observer, Pocock, were also killed. This left in the Squadron one original member, Geoffrey Hornblower Cock, who was destined to be shot down and taken prisoner in the following month. Captain Cock, one of the Squadrons leading aces, will be introduced later.

The first Camels arrived in July 1917, and by September the squadron was fully equipped and began operating successfully as a scout squadron. At the end of the year, the squadron transferred to the Austro-Italian front to carry out offensive patrols and ground attack sorties. In September 1918, the unit returned to France and joined the Independent Air Force as long-range escorts. It was intended to re-equip the squadron with specially modified Snipe for long range escort work, but these never materialized and it continued to operate Camels on normal fighter duties until the end of the war. The Independent Air Force (or Independent Force) will be further described under No. 110 Squadron, another Sedgeford-trained unit that served with this Force. 45 Squadron remained on the continent until February 1919, when it returned to the UK and disbanded at the turn of the year.

The squadron claimed 258 victories, including 164 enemy aircraft destroyed, during the war, the highest total for all the Sopwith-equipped units. The top ace, with 23 victories to his name, was Captain Matthew Brown Frew, who was awarded the Military Cross and Bar plus the Distinguished Service Order for conspicuous gallantry. Drew, who was not trained at Sedgeford, transferred to the RFC from the Highland Light Infantry in August 1916, and was posted to 45 Squadron in April 1917. He served in France and Italy and scored his victories flying the Squadron's Sopwith 1½ Strutters and Camels. In 1918 he was injured when his aircraft was hit by anti-aircraft fire. He returned to England and served as an instructor for the remainder of the war. He remained in the RAF, was knighted and retired with the rank of Air Vice-Marshal.

The second most successful ace was Australian Cedrick Ernest Howell DSO MC DFC. After serving as a sniper on the Western Front, Howell transferred to the Royal Flying Corps from 46 Battalion of the ANZAC. In 1917, he was assigned to 45 Squadron in France and served with this squadron in Northern Italy in 1918, scoring 19 victories as a Sopwith Camel pilot. Tragically, enroute back to Australia in December 1919, Howell was killed when the aircraft he was flying crashed into the sea near Corfu.

45 Squadron Combat Aircraft

The Sopwith 1½-Strutter was the first British fighter equipped with a fixed, forward-firing synchronised machine gun that could fire through the propeller. Many fighters of that time lacked the synchronisation mechanism and were called 'pushers' with the propeller mounted behind the fuselage and a machine gun mounted in the nose. In mid-1917, the Strutters were replaced by Sopwith Camels, an agile, highly maneouvrable biplane, generally regarded as one of the best fighters of the First World War.

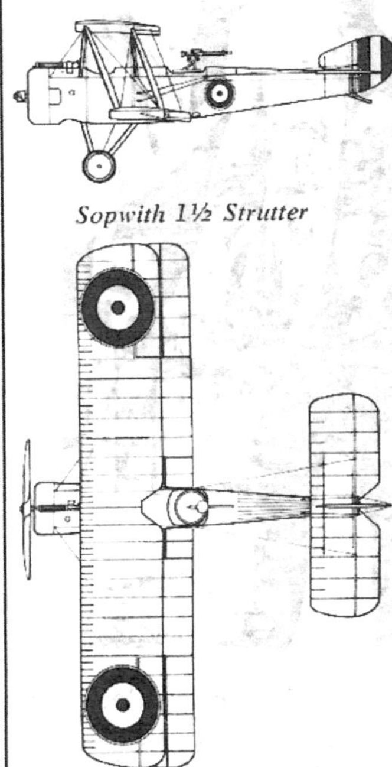

Sopwith 1½ Strutter

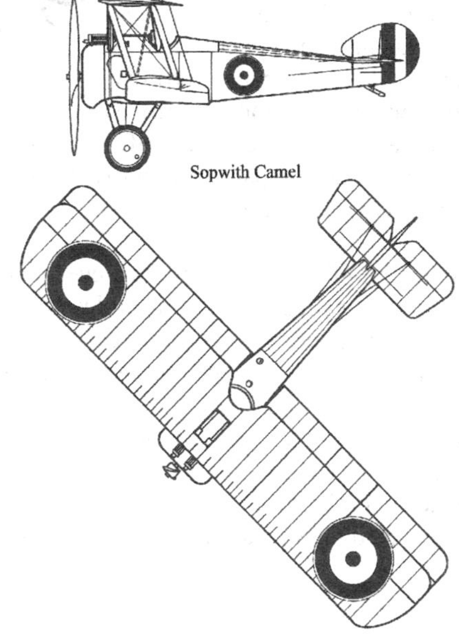

Sopwith Camel

The very successful Camel was so named because of the hump-shaped fairing over its two synchronised forward-firing machine guns. It was famous for its manoeuvrability and outstanding performance in battle, accounting for more aerial victories than any other allied aircraft in World War One..

Another notable 45 Squadron ace was 'B' Flight commander, Captain Geoffrey Hornblower Cock (Right), who began his elementary flying training with 25 Reserve Squadron at Thetford, joined 45 Squadron at Sedgeford in July 1916 to raise his flying to operational standard. He gained his 'wings' at Sedgeford in September 1916 and flew to France with the Squadron in mid October. He was later awarded the Military Cross for conspicuous gallantry and devotion to duty in France, only the second such award to be won by a pilot of 45 Squadron. Cross remained with the Squadron until 22 July 1917, when after 97 sorties against the enemy, he was shot down over enemy territory and spent the remainder of the war as a prisoner. Prior to his capture Cock had accounted for 19 enemy aircraft, the highest scoring ace flying the Sopwith 1½ Strutter. He was repatriated and remained in the Royal Air Force after the war, retiring as a Group Captain in 1943.

One of the minor aces, with five enemy aircraft to his name, was a young flight commander called Arthur Harris. During the Second World War, as Air Marshal Arthur 'Bomber' Harris, he became the legendary leader of RAF Bomber Command, who directed a strategic bombing campaign against Germany. This campaign controversially destroyed several German cities with huge numbers of civilian casualties. Harris joined 45 Squadron in 1917 as a flight commander in France. When he returned to England, Harris assumed command of No. 44 Squadron on home defence duties and was awarded the Air Force Cross. He later commanded 45 Squadron in the early 1920s, when they were serving in Iraq.

No. 64 Squadron RFC, later 64 Squadron RAF

No. 64 Squadron was formed at Sedgeford by redesignating an element of 45 Squadron on the 1st of August 1916 under its commanding officer Major B.E. Smythies, who was to retain command until December 1919. Initially the squadron conducted instructional flying using FE2b and BE2c aircraft. Many flying accidents occurred and several aircraft were wrecked during this period. The training involved exercises in conjunction with other units of 7 Wing, although, lacking good means of communication, opposing 'red' and 'blue' forces often failed to find each other and these exercises were not very successful.

The photograph on the right shows a close up of the nose of one of 64 Squadron's FE2bs.

Several fighter 'aces', with large numbers of enemy kills to their names, emerged from the fighting in France. One such hero was James B. McCudden MC, who visited Sedgeford as an instructor in May 1917 flying a Sopwith Pup from Wyton. He spent a few days instructing 64 Squadron in fighter tactics. He was well qualified, because he had been awarded his Military Cross for his bravery with 29 Squadron in France, where he had already accounted for several enemy aircraft. However, he was to get himself in trouble with his Commanding Officer at Sedgeford, as he later described.

"The weather up at Sedgeford was very hot, so there was not much flying during the day. One morning I went out to shoot hares with a .303 rifle, as the country up in Norfolk is overrun with them. I had some fun and managed to bag four hares and a partridge who, I must admit, was a sitter in more ways than one. When I got back to the Squadron, very pleased with my morning's bag, the CO was rather

angry, as from the game being out of season I had also been poaching. Oh! This weary world and all its troubles."

Captain McCudden was later appointed as a Flight Commander with 56 Squadron, flying SE5a aircraft in France. He was subsequently awarded the VC for his conspicuous bravery, accounting for 54 more enemy aircraft. After a four month rest spell in England, Major McCudden was ordered back to France to take command of 60 Squadron. On the 9th of July 1918, he crossed the Channel in his SE5a and landed at a French airfield to refuel before continuing to his new airfield. He took off again a few minutes later, but as he was climbing away his engine suddenly died. A few seconds later Major McCudden lay dead in the wreckage.

Back at Sedgeford in June 1917, 64 Squadron was re-designated a night flying training unit and began final preparations for France. In place of the earlier training aircraft, the squadron now received a flight of Henri Farmans and a flight of Sopwith Pups. Eventually, eighteen Airco DH5s were received, which were to be taken to France. The squadron began intensive training prior to its departure for France. This involved an air to ground gunnery course, low-level flying and cross-country formation flying. Gunnery practice was conducted over an area of salt marshes at nearby Thornham. Pilots from elementary training schools began their instruction on the Avro 504, which had twin dual control flying capability. They then progressed onto the Pup for solo work and finally onto the DH5s for the final period of training. Only the most promising and successful pilots were retained on the squadron strength. Others were eliminated at various points throughout the training schedule.

John A. Tyler wrote an excellent article in the Cross & Cockade International Journal Volume 8 Number 2 about the history of 64 Squadron at Sedgeford, which he called '*Norfolk Fledglings*'. In his article he highlights several flying accidents that occurred because of pilot inexperience and unreliable aircraft. One unfortunate trainee pilot, D. Redford, was involved in two accidents in as many days. First he had to make a forced landing in a corn field with his Farman, writing off the aircraft because of the severe damage to the wings and undercarriage. Luckily Redford was unharmed in this incident. The next day he stalled a Farman while landing it, causing the undercarriage to be driven through the wings and damaging the front spars. It is not clear whether Redford completed his training.

64 Squadron Training aircraft

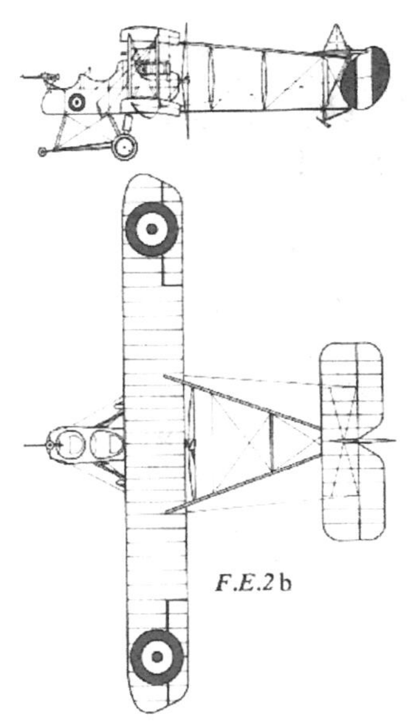

F.E.2b

The FE2b, manufactured by the Royal Aircraft Factory, was one of the first types to achieve broad success in several different roles. It was a pusher biplane powered by a 120 or 160 hp Beardmore engine. It was designed as a pusher, with the propeller pushing the aircraft from behind, to get round the problem of fitting a forward-firing machine gun, because at this time no interrupter or synchronising mechanism was available to allow the gun to be fired through the propeller. It was a two-seater carrying a pilot at the rear and an observer, who sat in the nose in front of the pilot. In the forward direction the FE2b had a fine arc of fire for the observer operating his machine gun. However, if it was attacked from the rear, the pilot had to stand up in his seat, holding the joystick between his knees and use his own gun, which fired backwards over the top of the upper wing. This was not easy, but it was frequently resorted to in a real dog fight.

The Sopwith Pup was officially known as the Sopwith Scout, but it was nicknamed 'Pup' because of its resemblance to the larger Sopwith 1½-Strutter. In addition to its training role, it was used on the Western front between September 1916 and late 1917. Its speed, supreme manoeuvrability and easy handling made it more than a match for most German fighters of the day.

The French Farman aircraft, jointly designed by the brothers Henri and Maurice Farman, were outdated by the time they came to Sedgeford. It was a 'pusher' type of aircraft, which was under-armed with its single nose mounted Lewis machine gun and small bomb carrying capacity.

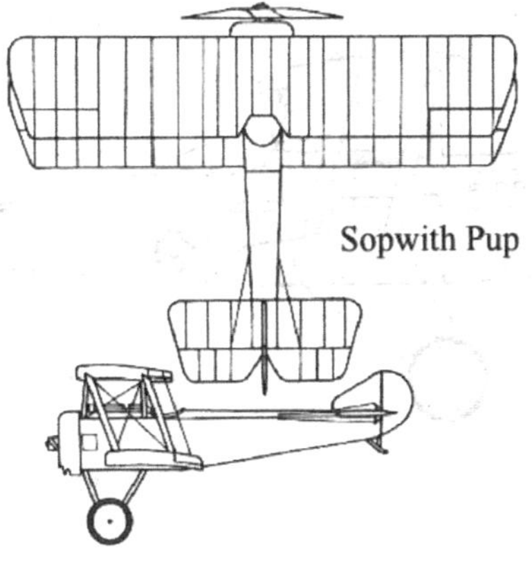

Sopwith Pup

64 Squadron Combat Aircraft

The Airco DH5, created by Geoffrey de Havilland, had an unusual design with the top wing staggered further back than the lower one, bringing the pilot's cockpit in front of the leading edge. This arrangement provided an excellent forward and upwards field of view, but tended to mask the all-important rearwards view, from which direction almost all attacks originated. It also proved too slow and lightly armed for operational combat and was very inefficient at high altitude. Consequently, it was not a particularly popular or successful front line aircraft, serving for only a few months between June 1917 and January 1918, when 64 Squadron was re-equipped with the SE5a, which had greater speed and a higher ceiling for operational flying.

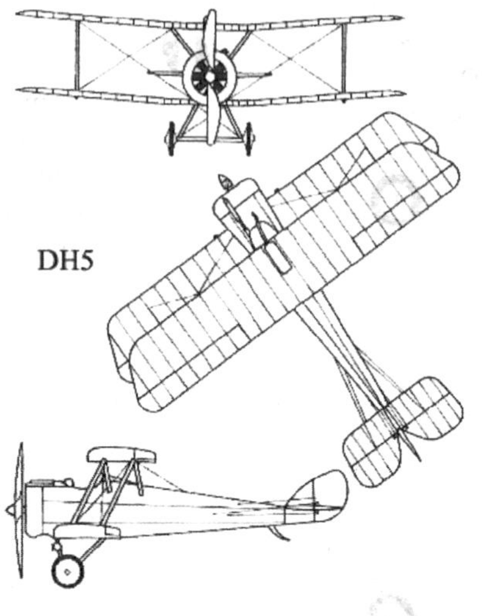

The SE5 and SE5a, manufactured by the Royal Aircraft Factory, were two of the best British fighter planes of the First World War. They were fast, tough and highly manoeuvrable, and proved to be more than a match for their German counterparts. They carried two fixed machine guns. One was synchronised to fire through the propeller, and the other was installed on the upper wing to fire over the propeller. Despite its frumpish appearance, pilots found that the S.E.5 was faster and had a higher ceiling than they had expected. Also its fuel capacity gave an endurance of two and a half hours, which was much longer than the German aircraft. So they were able to climb higher and stay there, waiting for the opposition to appear below them.

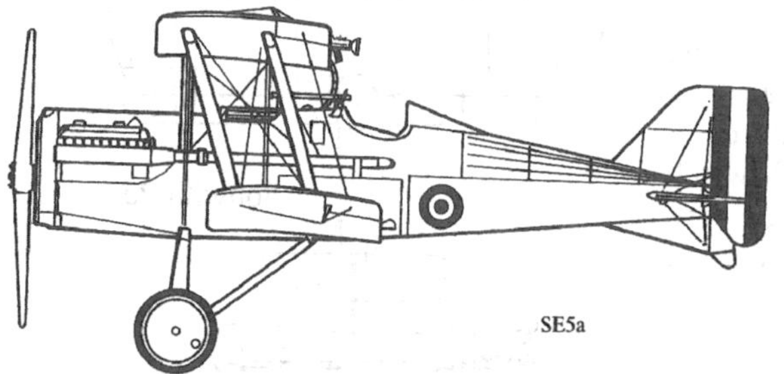

Three fatal accidents occurred during the final months of preparation for France.

This photograph shows a DH5 of 64 Squadron being prepared for take-off. This is the actual aircraft (A9393) that crashed, killing the Canadian pilot Captain E.G. Hanlan. He was killed at mid-day on July the 26th 1917 when his DH5 shed its upper starboard wing on completing a loop. The aircraft plunged into the ground at Bircham Newton, killing the pilot instantly.

Second Lieutenant A.L. Dean was badly injured on the afternoon of August the 8th when his aircraft, a Sopwith Pup, spun out of control and crashed near the Sedgeford to Docking road. He later died in King's Lynn Hospital and is buried in St. Mary's churchyard in Docking. In the third fatal accident Second Lieutenant F.B.H. Anderson was badly injured when his Sopwith Pup suffered an engine failure at 10,000 feet causing the aircraft to spin into the ground. Anderson died in King's Lynn Hospital five days later.

Tyler concluded that the squadron's Sopwith Pups seemed to have born the brunt of most accidents. This photograph shows one the Squadron's Sopwith Pups after a heavy landing at Sedgeford

Tyler also provided a nominal roll of 64 Squadron officers at 11 October 1917, which is reproduced in Appendix 2. The squadron commander, Major Bernard Edward Smythies, was to achieve the distinction of being the longest serving squadron commander during the war, commanding the squadron for two years and five months. He was subsequently awarded the DFC for his excellent leadership in January 1919. Major Smythies was supported by three flight commanders. The commander of B Flight was Captain R.S. McClintock, who had already served in France. Captain Edmund Roger Tempest commanded A Flight. Interestingly, he was brother to Wulstan Tempest, who famously downed Zeppelin L31 over Potters Bar on the 1st of October 1916. The Yorkshire-born Tempest brothers had emigrated to Canada to become farmers in Saskatchewan, but returned to England in 1914. C Flight was commanded by Captain James Anderson Slater, known as Jimmy, who would later return to Sedgeford to serve in No. 3 Fighting School. Jimmy Slater and Edmund Tempest would become the squadron's top aces in France, shooting down large numbers of enemy aircraft, known as 'victories'.

During its final days at Sedgeford, as a blessed relief from the meals in Docking Workhouse, where it had been billeted, the squadron enjoyed a farewell dinner cooked by Mr Everitt at the Hare Inn at Docking.

The squadron flew to France and the war on the morning of the 14th of October 1917. Eighteen aircraft departed from Sedgeford in squadron formation under the leadership of Major Smythies. Later in the morning the aircraft landed at Lympne on the Kent coast for a refuelling stop and then, in the afternoon, they proceeded over the channel to the Aircraft Depot at St Omer.

The St Omer Depot was the base through which all machines had to pass on their way to the Western Front. Squadrons landed there first, and then went on to their allotted aerodromes. 64 Squadron was attached to the 13th Wing, located on the 3rd Brigade front between Arras and Havincourt Wood. The squadron moved to Izel-le-Hameau (see Appendix 4) on the 15th of October and was soon heavily involved in ground strafing and low-level bombing duties during the Battle of Cambrai, suffering heavy casualties.

A report in *Chronicle of Aviation* for November 23 describes the action:

"British aircraft startled German troops today when they flew just a few feet above the Cambrai battlefield to clear the way for an allied advance by tanks and infantry. One pilot who cut through the dense mist and smoke recalled 'Ludicrous expressions of amazement on the upturned faces of German troops as we passed a few feet above their trenches.' With German airmen grounded by fog and totally outnumbered, DH5s of No. 64 Squadron of Britain's RFC, whose members have practiced low flying in England, provoked panic with their concerted attack on the German lines ..."

Many believe that this battle signalled the birth of mechanised warfare, when hundreds of British tanks were used as an independent force for the first time. The aircraft were used in a supporting role strafing enemy positions. Although the tanks succeeded in breaking through the enemy lines, the Germans eventually regained much of the ground they had earlier lost in this battle.

In January 1918 the squadron's DH5s were replaced by SE5As and some weeks were spent performing conversion training. The pilots soon began to appreciate the increase in speed and greater operational altitude of the SE5a and began to shoot down enemy aircraft in earnest in a new fighter role.

The 23rd of March was a red-letter day for the squadron when eight 'victories' were scored, intensifying the competition between Captains Slater and Tempest for the top scoring pilot of the squadron. Both of these aces downed two more aircraft each on this eventful day. After March 1918, the war intensified for 64 Squadron, reaching a peak in August of that year when it flew more than 1130 hours. During its time in France, the squadron received credit for seventy two aircraft destroyed, sixty three shot down out of control, and one balloon shot down in flames, making a total of 136 victories, which are itemised in Appendix 3. Captain Jimmy Slater, who was awarded the MC and Bar and the DFC, was the squadron's leading ace with more than 20 victories. The second-ranking ace was Captain Edmund Tempest, who was also awarded the MC and DFC.

The squadron returned to England in February 1919 as cadre-only (without aircraft) and was disbanded at Narborough at the end of the year.

No. 53 Reserve Squadron, later 53 Training Squadron

No. 53 Reserve Squadron, which was later renamed 53 Training Squadron, was formed at Sedgeford on the first of February 1917 by re-designating an element of 64 Squadron. It was equipped with several aircraft types, including an RE8, a BE2c, an Avro 504J and a DH6. The Squadron moved on to Narborough a few days later.

No. 65 Reserve Squadron, later 65 Training Squadron

No. 65 Reserve Squadron, which had formed at Croydon on the 1st of May 1917, came to Sedgeford a few days later and was renamed 65 Training Squadron. The squadron had a number of different types of training aircraft, including Avro 504A, BE2e, RE8, Bristol Scout, and others. It left Sedgeford in late November 1917.

The RE8 reconnaissance bomber

The twin-seat RE8, produced by the Royal Aircraft Factory, was developed to replace the BE2 series of aircraft and was heavily used as a training aircraft and reconnaissance bomber on the Western Front. Although somewhat unstable and difficult to fly, it was well armed with one Lewis and one Vickers machine gun.

Nicknamed 'Harry Tate', after a popular music hall performer, by the RAF and RFC airmen of the day, it was Britain's most widely used two-seater during WWI. 15 RAF Squadrons were still flying the RE8 at the time of the Armistice.

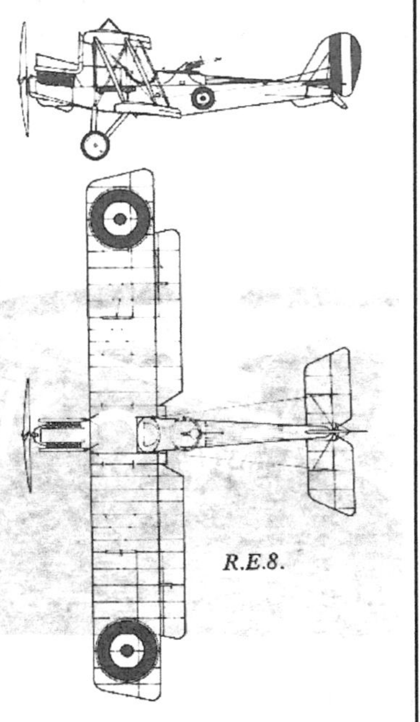

No. 87 Squadron RFC, later 87 Squadron RAF

No. 87 Squadron, under the command of Captain C.J.W. Darwin, arrived from Upavon in the middle of September 1917 and stayed for four months preparing for its transfer to the war zone in France. For training it used Avro 504, SE5 and Sopwith Pup aircraft types. 87 Squadron moved on to Hounslow in mid December 1917 to re-equip with Sopwith Dolphin aircraft, which it delivered to France as replacement aircraft for the Dolphin squadrons operating there.

The Dolphin's introduction was marred by several incidents in which allied pilots attacked the new aircraft, mistaking it for a German type. For the next few weeks, Dolphin pilots had to exercise caution near other allied aircraft. New pilots also voiced concern over the Dolphin's wing arrangement, fearing serious injury to the head and neck in the event of a crash. Early aircraft were often fitted with improvised crash pylons over the cockpit to protect the pilot's head. Despite these problems, the Dolphin proved successful and generally popular with pilots, being fast, maneouvrable and easy to fly, although some pilots were disoriented by the fact that the nose of the aircraft was not visible from the cockpit. The Dolphin performed particularly well at high altitude. For this reason, Dolphins were often deployed against German reconnaissance aircraft. The photograph shows a Dolphin of 87 Squadron with a Lewis gun mounted on top of the lower right wing panel.

The squadron returned to England to re-equip with SE5A aircraft prior to its return to France in April 1918, when the German offensive was at its peak. By the Armistice it had downed 89 enemy aircraft.

No. 72 Squadron RFC, later 72 Squadron RAF

No. 72 Squadron formed at Netheravon in early July 1917 from a nucleus provided by the Central Flying School. It moved to Sedgeford in November 1917, under the command of Major H.W. von Poelnitz, and mobilised for operations in Mesopotamia, leaving on Christmas Day and regrouping in Basra on the 2nd of March 1918. It became 72 Squadron RAF from the 1st of April 1918 whilst in Mesopotamia (now called Iraq). Here, the unit operated as self-contained Flights allotted to individual Army Corps. 'A' Flight, with DH4, SE5a and Spad planes, went to Samarra with 1 Corps; 'B' Flight with Martinsydes went to Baghdad; and 'C' Flight, with Bristol monoplanes went to Mirjan to work with 3 Corps.

Bristol M.1C

The M.IC was a powerful single-seat monoplane fighter that could reach a speed of 130 mph and had an operational ceiling of 20,000 feet. Although it was potentially one of the finest aircraft of its day, the M1.C suffered from prejudice against monoplanes in a time when biplanes were considered safer and more reliable. Consequently, it only saw action in Macedonia, Palestine and Mesopotamia, where it was used by No. 72 Squadron.

They were used mainly in the ground attack role where they mesmerized the opposition. On one occasion two M.1C pilots of 'C' Flight put up such a fearsome display of aerobatics that a complete Kurdish tribe was persuaded to defect to the allies.

While 'C' Flight was involved in its ground attack role with 3 Corps, 'B' Flight was involved with a force trying to break through to the Caspian, to prevent the Turks from taking over Persia. This involved moving with the troops, making its own airfields in the mountains as it went. Their Martinsydes were kept very busy bombing and strafing enemy positions. 'A' Flight's main action took place in

October, when it took part in operations to surround the Turks on the Tigris front. This also involved ground attack sorties.

The reader may be confused by the many battles that were fought in Mesopotamia during the First World War. These actions include epic struggles fought along the banks of the River Tigris. They started with an unstoppable advance by the British throughout 1915 followed by a resurgence of the Turkish opposition in 1916, culminating in the British defeat during the Siege of Kut in April 1916, when the British suffered 23,000 casualties and 8,000 soldiers were taken prisoner by the Ottomans. However, British fortunes revived again with the appointment of Sir Frederick Stanley Maude as regional Commander-in-Chief, and finally led to complete British victory in the region in October 1918, when General Marshall (Maude's successor) accepted the surrender of the Turkish 6th Army under the command of Khalil Pasha. 72 Squadron played a major part in this British victory, supporting the army corps involved.

Following the surrender of the Turks, 72 Squadron set sail for the UK, in February 1919, disbanding in September.

No. 110 Squadron RFC, later 110 Squadron RAF

No. 110 Squadron RFC was formed at Rendcombe in Gloucestershire on the 1st of November 1917, but moved to Sedgeford a few days later equipped with various types of training aircraft. It became 110 Squadron RAF from the 1st of April 1918 whilst at Sedgeford.

The squadron trained in preparation for its transfer to France, but this was delayed because of the non-availability of suitable aircraft. Replacement DH4s and DH9s were received but deemed to be unsuitable for the task. Eventually, in June 1918, the squadron moved to Kenley to enable it to re-equip with the more capable DH9As, in preparation for transfer to France at the beginning of September.

One of 110 Squadron's DH9As

The squadron joined a bomber force known as the Independent Air Force, or Independent Force, under the command of Major General Hugh Trenchard, comprising several day and night bombing squadrons plus a fighter escort squadron based at several airfields around Nancy in France. Interestingly, the fighter escort squadron was the Sedgeford-trained 45 Squadron, flying Sopwith Camel aircraft. The unfortunately named Independent Force, which was created in May 1918, to work directly under the Air Ministry, was tasked with conducting a strategic bombing campaign against Germany. It took the war to German cities like Frankfurt, Cologne and Mannheim for the last five months of the war.

Consequently, for the remainder of the war, 110 Squadron was employed on long-distance day bombing raids against targets in Germany with DH9A aircraft - the first squadron to employ this aircraft.

Airco DH9A Bomber

The DH9A bomber was a replacement for its predecessors, the DH4 and DH9, but its entry into the war was delayed until August 1918 because of engine problems. Part of this delay was due to the non-availability of the American-built Liberty engines. Eventually, unlike its predecessors, the DH9A gained a reputation for reliability. Although nominally a conversion of the earlier aircraft types, to take the more reliable American engine, the new DH9A was changed in many aspects. By the end of 1918 nearly nine-hundred had been built.

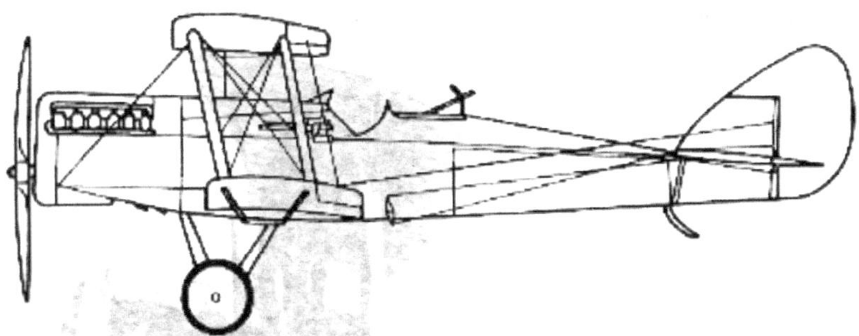

The aircraft carried a crew of two - a pilot and a gunner. For defensive armament the DH9A possessed one fixed, synchronised machine gun in the nose, and one or two Lewis guns in the gunner's cockpit. It could also carry a bomb load 230 lbs to distant targets.

The DH9A continued in RAF service going on to form the backbone of the Royal Air Force's post-war colonial bombing force, and surviving until the 1930s.

The squadrons original complement of DH9As were the gift of His Serene Highness the Nizam of Hyderabad. Each aircraft bore an inscription to that effect and the unit became known as the Hyderabad Squadron.

Peter Chapman wrote an article, *'Frankfurt – By Night and Day'*, giving two accounts of the long distance bombing of Frankfurt. One of these accounts describes a daylight operation performed by 110 Squadron on the 25th of September 1918, less than one month after they joined the Independent Force. The Squadron had already received a baptism of fire in the middle of the month, when it had attacked Mannheim and lost two aircraft over the target.

On this occasion, thirteen available aircraft were called upon to attack Frankfurt. The first flight of seven aircraft was led by Captain A Lindley and the second flight of six aircraft was led by Captain A.C.H. Groom. They took off around 10 AM and crossed into German territory without incident. However, shortly after 11:15, the formation was surprised by a large group of German aircraft, losing two of the DH9As. The remainder pressed on to bomb their target, which was Frankfurt's main railway station. Although they dropped a total of one and a half tons of bombs, most missed the station by about half a mile, scattering across other parts of the city. One person was killed and seven people were injured by the falling bombs and minor property damage was caused. On the return journey, the two flights got separated and were both attacked by enemy aircraft, losing two more aircraft.

In all, four aircraft failed to return. Two aircraft and their four crewmen were forced down in Germany and made prisoners, while two aircraft were shot down and their four crewmen killed. Although 110 Squadron had tried its best to carry out the assigned mission, it had been ruthlessly exposed over German territory. Although it had done some damage to Frankfurt, and had claimed to have shot down a number of enemy aircraft, it was a very poor return for all the sacrifices that had been made.

The squadron lost another seven aircraft out of a formation of 13 on the 21st of October, when they were again attacked on the way to Frankfurt. On this occasion, none of the bombers reached their target. In addition to these losses during the three daylight raids on Frankfurt in 1918, many other aircraft returned in a damaged condition with dead and wounded on board.

No. 110 Squadron was disbanded on the 27th of August 1919 at Marquise, France.

No. 122 Squadron RFC, later 122 Squadron RAF

No. 122 Squadron was formed at Sedgeford on the 1st of January 1918 as a training squadron, becoming 122 Squadron RAF on the 1st of April. It was planned that it would mobilize as a day bomber unit for deployment to France with DH9 aircraft. It began training on a variety of aircraft types but had not become operational before it disbanded in August.

This photograph shows one of 122 Squadron's Sopwith Camel training aircraft. Note the lucky charm swastika painted on the tail fin.

No. 9 Training Squadron

No. 9 Training Squadron arrived from Mousehold Heath, Norwich on the 10th of January with DH4 aircraft, staying until August. Mousehold Heath had an interesting connection with Norfolk's aviation industry. One of the other units based there during WWI was No 3 Aircraft Acceptance Park, its task being to accept into service aircraft manufactured by several local companies, including Boulton & Paul and Mann, Egerton & Co of Norwich. Squadrons sometimes collected replacement aircraft from Mousehold Heath.

Other Royal Air Force Squadrons

The three previous flying units, **110 Squadron**, **122 Squadron** and **9 Training Squadron,** were serving at Sedgeford when the RAF came into being in April 1918. Other squadrons were later to arrive for short periods of time, including **60 Squadron RAF**, which arrived from France without aircraft in February 1919 before moving on to Narborough; and **13 Squadron RAF**, also reduced to cadre, which arrived from France in March 1919 and remained until it disbanded at the end of the year.

No. 3 Fighting School

No. 3 School of Aerial Fighting and Gunnery was formed at Driffield in Yorkshire in early May 1918, moving south during the same month to Bircham Newton, where it was re-designated No. 3 Fighting School. In October 1918, the school moved to Sedgeford. It had a wide variety of aircraft at its disposal, including a BE2a, DH4, DH5, DH9, DH9A, SE5a, F2b, Avro 504K, Sopwith Snipe, Sopwith Camel and others. The school was re-designated as 7 Training Squadron on the 14th of March 1919 and was disbanded in October 1919.

Norman Franks wrote in the Cross & Cockade Journal Volume 8 Number 2 about the previously mentioned 64 Squadron WWI fighter Ace, Jimmy Slater, who was awarded the Military Cross and bar as well as the Distinguished Flying Cross for his exploits in France, which included more than 20 victories (downed enemy aircraft). Captain Slater joined 3 Fighting School as an instructor at the end of his final tour of duty in France in July 1918. It was Slater's second posting to Sedgeford, where he had commanded 64 Squadron's C Flight during training at the aerodrome prior to the Squadron departing for France in 1917.

Captain Slater MC DFC

Slater clearly enjoyed his period as an instructor at Sedgeford, particularly those opportunities he would have to perform spectacular aerobatics. One trick was to fly through one end of a hanger and out the other end. Once he was asked to perform a solo display for Queen Alexandra during her visit to the aerodrome from Sandringham. Apparently The Queen soon turned to the Commanding Officer and said '*Order that young man down before he kills himself*'. Another of Slater's favourite sports was to beat up the town of Hunstanton at chimney pot height visiting each of his girlfriend's houses in turn. Fortunately Jimmy Slater survived his antics at Sedgeford and was subsequently granted a permanent commission in the Royal Air Force. Tragically his luck ran out in 1925, when he was killed in a flying accident while serving at the Central Flying School at Upavon.

Flying accidents were also common at No. 3 Fighting School. On the 24th of January 1919, two of the school's Sopwith Camels collided causing one of them to crash, killing the pilot, Captain C.F. King MC DFC. The other aircraft, piloted by a South African, Second Lieutenant Hector Daniel MC, landed safely. Captain King was buried in St. Mary's churchyard in Docking.

Captain C.F. King MC DFC

Cecil Frederick King, who previously served in France flying Sopwith Camels with 43 Squadron, was an ace credited with destroying 22 enemy aircraft. He was awarded the Military Cross in April 1918 for conspicuous gallantry and devotion to duty. He was later awarded the Distinguished Flying Cross in August 1918 for his leadership and gallantry. 2/Lt Daniel, the surviving pilot involved in King's fatal accident, also served in France with 43 Squadron and was decorated with the Military Cross. He was an ace with nine victories to his name. He joined the South African Air Force in 1923 and rose to Brigadier rank before he retired in 1953. Tragically he later committed suicide in a Pretoria hospital.

The Commanding Officer of 3 Fighting School was Cecil King's former 43 Squadron Flight Commander in France and close friend, Major Harold Harington Balfour MC and bar, an ace with 9 victories to his name. Balfour joined the School at Driffield, before moving it to Bircham Newton and then to Sedgeford. Balfour claimed the dubious honour of being the first man to fly naked over Hunstanton, a feat he performed after nude bathing at a remote beach near Brancaster. After leaving the RAF, Balfour entered politics and became a conservative politician in 1929. In 1938 he was appointed Under Secretary of State for Air, a position he held throughout WW2. He gained the title of 1st Baron Balfour of Inchrye in 1945.

Other Recollections

Mr. Alan Garfitt, from Soham, near Ely, supplied the following photograph taken on the day that his father, Rush Garfitt, and mother, Florence, were married in Docking Church, on the 7th of May 1918.

The photograph was taken outside Field Barn Cottages, almost opposite the site of Sedgeford aerodrome. The newly married couple are shown seated in the centre of the group. Rush, who was from Yorkshire, was a fully qualified boot and shoe maker, a trade he practiced at Sedgeford as a member of the Royal Flying Corps and the Royal Air Force. Florence was a cook in the Women's Royal Army Corps. After the war they settled in Sedgeford, and for many years Mr Garfitt was the Secretary of the Sedgeford Branch of the Royal British Legion. The three other ladies on the photograph were sisters of the bride. The elderly couple, Mr and Mrs Smith, were tenants in the cottage. Unfortunately, the identity of the two other airmen, who were probably acting as witnesses, is not known.

Mr. Garfitt also informed the author about a Mrs Drewery, who kept an open house, known as *'Avro House'*, where the airmen from Sedgeford could relax during their off-duty periods. This was at one end of a row of cottages adjacent to the Plough public house. Apparently the old pub (now closed) and cottages are on the opposite side of the road to the distinctive 'Magazine House', which is situated at the Docking end of the village. Mr W. Garfitt, from Heacham, supplied additional photographs, which are shown overleaf.

Naval Airmen at Sedgeford in 1916

Royal Flying Corps personnel at Sedgeford

Sedgeford Aeroplanes

De Havilland DH4

BE2s

Avro 504 Trainer

Footnotes

1. Sedgeford aerodrome, like Narborough, was a victim of the huge reductions made to the RAF during the post-war period, closing in 1920.

2. In a separate survey conducted towards the end of World War One, four of Norfolk's major airfields were considered for their suitability for use by the new Handley Page V/1500 long-range bombers. Sedgeford, Narborough and Pulham were deemed to be inferior to Bircham Newton for this purpose, and Bircham was selected as the new home for these bombers. In the report of this survey, produced by Lt. Col. R.H. Mulock in July 1918, Sedgeford was found to be unsuitable on account of the sloping ground and the amount of reconstruction which would be necessary to put the facilities in order. The V/1500s were subsequently housed at Bircham Newton, and No. 3 Fighting School was moved to Sedgeford to make way for them, but the Armistice was signed before these large bombers saw any action.

3. It is necessary to address the local myth that Lord Mountbatten - the great grandson of Queen Victoria and cousin to King George V - learned to fly at Sedgeford. This seems very unlikely when one considers Mountbatten's busy life in the period (1915–1920) when Sedgeford was operational. From January 1915 until mid 1916 he attended the Royal Naval College at Osborne; he then went to sea with the Royal Navy until late 1919; from October 1919 he was an undergraduate at Cambridge; and from March until October 1920 he accompanied the Prince of Wales (later King Edward VIII) on an official trip to Australia and New Zealand. Although one cannot rule out unofficial visits to Sedgeford, on occasions when he may have visited Sandringham, there is no evidence that he trained at Sedgeford. On the contrary, in his Mountbatten biography, Philip Ziegler provides compelling evidence that Mountbatten learned to fly at Hamble in 1930, when he was serving as a Royal Naval instructor at Portsmouth. This was long after Sedgeford had closed.

4. Second Lieutenant H.G.R. Boyt died in a crash of a DH4 from Sedgeford on 31st of August 1918 and is buried in Stanhoe churchyard Also, Second Lieutenant James Alan Pearson of the Royal Flying Corps, who died on the 9th of December 1917, is buried in St. Mary's churchyard in Docking. No further information about these deceased officers is available at the time of writing.

The Aerodrome during World War I

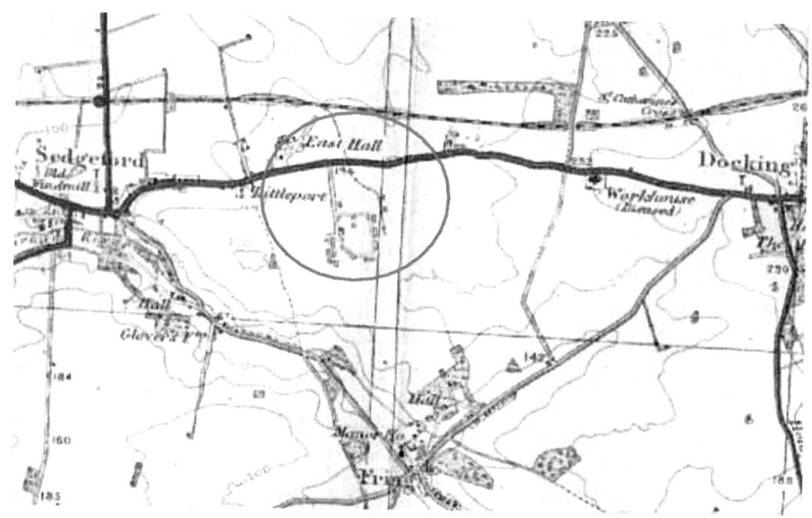

The site covered 170 acres about one mile east of Sedgeford village on the south side of the Docking road near East Hall as shown on this map segment. It possessed three large hangers as well as canvas hangers and other buildings. The site also had its own railhead, which connected to the Heacham to Wells-next-the-Sea branch line.

Artist impression of the aerodrome showing canvas hangers

Lt. Col. R.N. Mulock and Major Allsop, from the newly formed RAF Independent Force, visited Sedgeford in 1918, when they evaluated several airfields to see if they were suitable for the new Handley Page V/1500 bomber. In their report, dated 19/7/18, they described the facilities at Sedgeford as follows:

"The surface here is good but the ground slopes away from the sheds to the borders of the aerodrome. This might prove a slight difficulty with the wind in certain directions....There are 3 large Hangers approx 150 ft. by 50 ft. by 20 ft. high. There are also 4 double small hangers which are of no use for housing large machines, but which would be useful in the capacity of workshops. There is permanent accommodation for some 100 officers and 200 men and new quarters are under construction..... The workshops are small and need enlargement.... Water is laid on throughout the station and in the sheds. An electric power station is installed here also."

The old Docking workhouse

Because the aerodrome did not possess sufficient accommodation, some messing and sleeping facilities were provided in the disused Docking workhouse, which was described as being damp and uncomfortable.

No. 65 Squadron RFC
vertical recce photo of
Sedgeford Aerodrome
12 Oct 1917

This aerial view was taken by No. 65 Squadron RFC in October 1917. Many buildings, including a large hanger and several canvas hangers and equipment sheds are shown to the area to the south of the plantation known as Whin Close.

Mr. Michael Hudson, whose maternal grandparents both served at Sedgeford, identified the large hanger as a Belfast Truss type, as indicated by the shadow of a curved roof. Michael also identified the other long building towards the south-west corner of the photograph as a mess with two well-trodden entrances. Below the mess, on the end closest to the large hanger, is a cookhouse with a large flue on the south-west end.

The Former Aerodrome in World War II

The former aerodrome at Sedgeford became one of RAF Bircham Newton's decoy sites during World War Two. The existing buildings at that time were used to create a 'K' site, or dummy airfield, with dummy aircraft and a false runway that could be lit up at night to divert enemy aircraft away from Bircham Newton. The decoy site contained an underground bunker, where the airmen could shelter during a raid. The site was attacked at least once, when a German aircraft machine gunned the site.

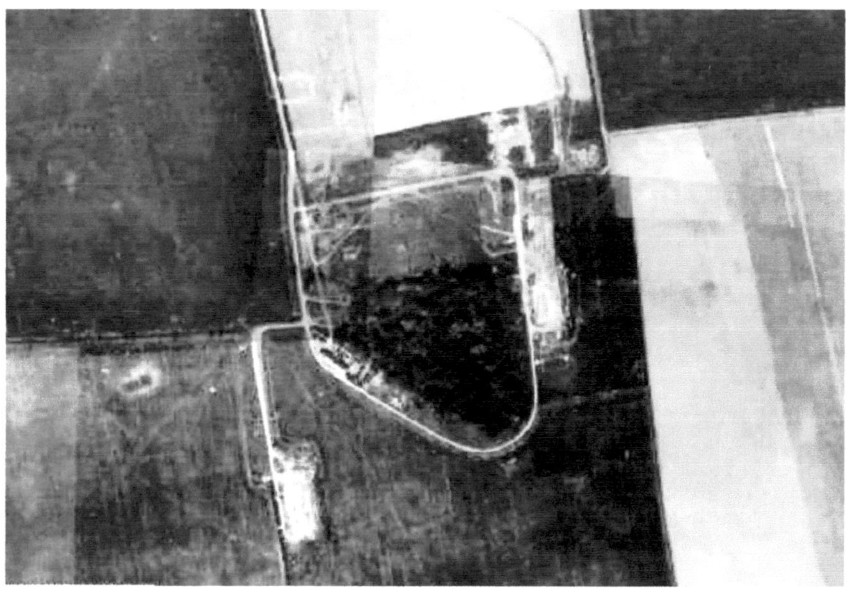

This aerial photograph, taken at the end of WW2, shows that many of the original aerodrome buildings were still standing at that time. Others, like the large hanger to the south-west of Whin Close, had been dismantled but the foundations were still visible.

The Former Aerodrome Today

A few dilapidated buildings survive at Sedgeford, but little remains to identify it as a former First World War aerodrome.

This 2007 Google Earth image shows some of the remaining buildings, but nature and farming are obviously reclaiming the site.

The following photographs, recently taken by the author on a foggy morning, show some building remains, including the underground bunker created during WW2.

Appendix 1

45 Squadron's Initial Operational Establishment

Executives

Maj W R Read (OC No 45 Sqn)
Capt G Mountford (OC A Flt)
Capt E F P Lubbock (OC B Flt)
Capt L Porter (OC C Flt)

Pilots

Lt L W McArthur
Lt C S J Griffin
Lt L A Chamier
2/Lt H G P Lowe
2/Lt E G Manuel
2/Lt H H Griffith
2/Lt M J Fenwick
2/Lt G H Cock
2/Lt V B Allen
2/Lt O J Wade
2/Lt G H Rodwell
2/Lt N H Read
2/Lt E E Glorney
2/Lt L F Jones
F/Sgt W G Webb
Sgt R G Malcolm
Sgt P Snowden

Observers

Lt F Surgey
2/Lt G H Bennett
2/Lt W J Thuell
2/Lt A S Carey
2/Lt N G Arnold
2/Lt C S Emery
2/Lt W Jordan
2/Lt F H Austin
2/Lt G B Samuels
2/Lt J A Vessey
2/Lt F Fullerton
2/Lt D E Greenhow
Sgt P S Taylor

Ground Staff

Lt R C Morgan (Rec Off)
2/Lt L R Wright (W/T Off)
2/Lt T H Birdsall (AEO)

Appendix 2

64 Squadron Aircraft and Officers (November 1917)

The individual aircraft used by 64 Squadron together with a nominal roll for 11 November 1917 are provided below. 64 Squadron was organised as a typical RFC squadron, comprising an Officer Commanding, who would normally be a pilot of Major rank, and three flights (A, B and C), each commanded by a Captain. In addition, there would be a Recording Officer, responsible for the Orderly Room, an Armament Officer, to maintain all personal and aircraft arms, and an Equipment Officer, responsible for the ordering, accounting and issuing of equipment. One would normally also find a Transport Officer, responsible for the maintenance of vehicles, and an HQ Officer, responsible for maintenance, cooking and special tasks. These latter appointments are not visible on this nominal roll for October 1917.

Major B E Smythies	Royal Engineers	Sqn Commander
Capt R St C	Royal Field	B Flight Commander
McClintock	Artillery	B Flight Commander
Capt J A Slater	Royal Flying Corps	C Flight Commander
Capt E R Tempest	Royal Flying Corps	A Flight Commander
Capt H J Petty	Welsh Regt	Flying Officer B Flt
Capt A C St C Morford	Royal Marine Light Infantry	Flying Officer A Flt
Capt H T Fox-Russell	Royal Welsh Fusiliers	Flying Officer C Flt
Lt A A Duffuss	Royal Field Artillery	Flying Officer B Flt
Lt R C Hardie	Duke of Cornwalls Light Infantry	Flying Officer B Flt
Lt R E Angus	Ayreshire Yeomanry	Flying Officer A Flt
Lt J A V Boddy	Durham Light Infantry	Flying Officer B Flt
Lt L B Williams	Royal Flying Corps	Flying Officer B Flt
Lt J P McRae	Canadian Army Service Corps	Flying Officer A Flt
Lt P S Burge	Royal Flying Corps	Flying Officer C Flt
2Lt S W Poore	Royal Flying Corps	Flying Officer A Flt
Lt F H Parker	Royal Flying Corps	Flying Officer C Flt
2Lt O W Meredith	Royal Flying Corps	Flying Officer A Flt
Lt C I B Voge	Royal Flying Corps	Flying Officer C Flt
2Lt E E Ashton	Royal Flying Corps	Flying Officer C Flt
Lt K G P Hendrie	Royal Flying Corps	Flying Officer C Flt
Lt R Turner	Royal Flying Corps	Recording Officer
Lt R W V Midland	Kings Royal Rifles	Armament Officer
2Lt A Miller	Royal Flying Corps	Equipment Officer

Appendix 3

VICTORIES SCORED BY THE PILOTS OF No.64 SQUADRON. R.F.C./R.A.F.

PILOT	DESTROYED	O.O.C.	TOTAL.
Capt. J.A. Slater, M.C. & Bar, D.F.C.	11½	9	20½
Capt. E.R. Tempest, M.C., D.F.C.	11	3	14
Capt. P.S. Burge, M.C.	7½	2	9½
Capt. W.H. Farrow, D.F.C.	5	4	9
Lt. T. Rose, D.F.C.	4	5	9
Capt. D. Lloyd-Evans, D.F.C.	5	3	8
Capt. C. Cudemore	2	6	8
Capt. E.D. Atkinson, D.F.C.	3	2	5
Lt. B.A. Walkerdine	2	3	5
Capt. R.S.C. McClintock, M.C.	3	2	5
Squadron Patrols	2	3	5
Lt. M.L. Howard	3	1	4
Sgt. A.S. Cowlishaw	3	1	4
Lt. C. Bisonette	1	2	3
Lt. A.G. Donald	1	2	3
Lt. J.F.T. Barrett	1	2	3
Lt. A.A. Duffus	—	2	2
Lt. V.W. Thompson	—	2	2
Lt. W.R. Henderson	1	1	2
Lt. A.C. Hendry, M.C.	1	1	2
Lt. G. Wood	—	2	2
2Lt. R.H. Topliss	—	1	1
Lt. I.M. Harris	1	—	1
Lt. W.C. Daniel	1	—	1
Lt. G.A. Rainier	—	1	1
Lt. H.G. Ross	1	—	1
Lt. G.W. Schermerhorn	—	1	1
Capt. A.F. Buck	—	1	1
Capt. F.J. Gibbs	1	—	1
Lt. H.C. Hayes	1*	—	1*
Lt. A.H.B. Youell	1	—	1
Lt. L.E. Bickel	—	1	1
* Balloon. Totals:	73	63	136

Appendix 4

Maps of the Western Front

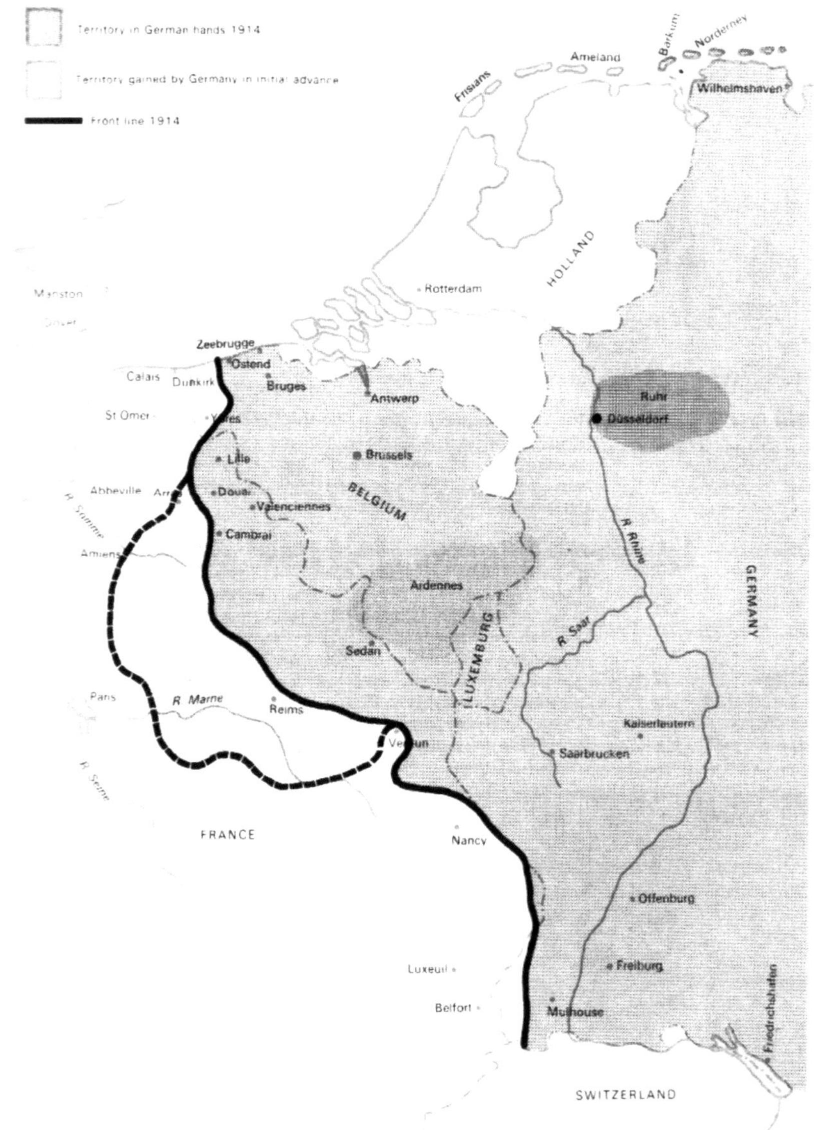

The following map shows 45 Squadron's airfield at St Marie Cappel, near the small town of Cassel, between St Omer and Ypres. It also shows 64 Squadron's airfield at Izel Le Hameau, midway between St Pol and Arras.

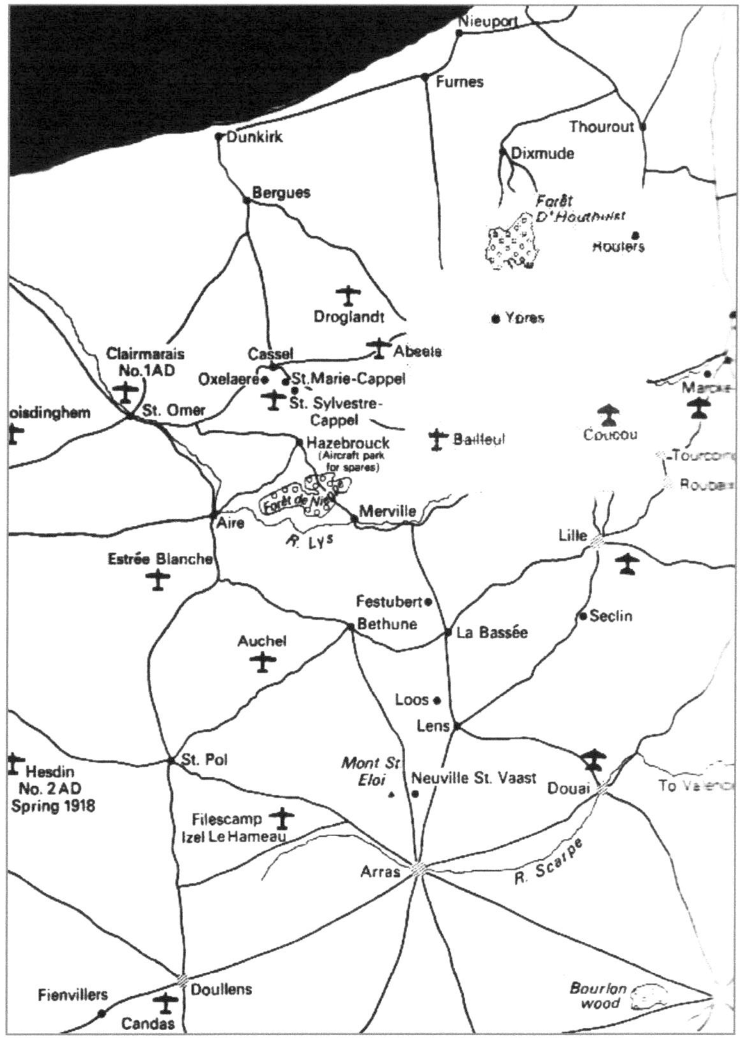

Please note that map details have been removed from the main battle area around Ypres.

Appendix 5

Units that served at Sedgeford and their Aircraft

Unit	Arrival	Departure	Types of Aircraft
45 Squadron	12 May 1916 from Thetford	4 October 1916 to France	Sopwith 1½ Strutter (Sep 1916–Sep 1917) e.g. 7774, 7792, A1075, A1083, A2381, A8260, B2576, B2583 Nieuport Two Seater (April 1917-May 1917) Sopwith Camel (July 1917–Feb 1919} e.g. B2314, B2321, B2376, B2430, B3871, B3903, B4607, B5181, B6238, B6383, B6412, B7381
64 Squadron	Formed at Sedgeford on 1 Aug 1916	14 October 1917 to France	Airco DH5 (Jun 1917-Mar 1918) e.g. A9177, A9507, A9458 SE5a (Jan 1918-Feb 1919) e.g. B2, B125, C6418, C6447, D289, D6900
53 Training Squadron	Formed at Sedgeford on 1 Feb 1917	14 Feb 1917 to Narborough	RE8, BE2e (B9998), 504J (B957), DH6 (B2667)
65 Training Squadron	10 May 1917 from Croydon	25 Nov 1917 to Dover	FK3 (A1494), FK8 (B297) Scout D (A1779), Camel BE2d (6734), BE2e (B790) Elephant (A3995), RE8 (A3486) 504A (A8585), 504J (B956)
87 Squadron	Mid Sept 1917 from Upavon	Mid Dec 1917 to Hounslow	5F1 Dolphin (Dec 1917- Feb 1919) e.g. C3778, C4056, C4159, C4176, C4230, C8072, C8197, D3671, D3764, D5231, E4434, E4493 SE5A (April 1918-) e.g. D305
72 Squadron	November 1917 from Netheravon	25 Dec 1917 to Mesopotamia	Martinsyde G.100 (Dec 1917-Nov 1918} Spad S.7 (Mar 1918-Nov 1918) e.g. A8802, A8806, A8808, A8810 Bristol M.1c (Mar 1918-Nov 1918) SE5a (Mar 1918-Nov 1918)
110 Squadron	November 1917 from Rendcombe	June 1918 to Kenley	BE2d, BE2e, RE8, DH6, Elephant, FK8 DH9 e.g. D3117 DH9A e.g. F1000 (from mid 1918)
122 Squadron	Formed at Sedgeford on 1 Jan 1918	Disbanded at Sedgeford on 17 August 1918	DH9 proposed, but used various aircraft until it was disbanded
9 Training Squadron	10 Jan 1918 from Norwich	August 1918 to Tallaght	Shorthorn (2468), Longhorn (4013), Caudron GIII (5038) 504 (799), FE2b (6963) FE2d (A6361), H Farman (719) BE2c (2718), BE2e (A3111) FB5 (5665), Martinsyde S1 (4249) RE8 (A3921), DH4 (A7662) FK3 (A8126)
3 Fighting School	November 1918 from Bircham Newton	Re-designated 7 Training Squadron on 14 Mar 1919	Kangaroo, 0/400 (F248) BE2c (6786), Camel (H2724 '9') DH4 (B2100), DH9 (D7332) DH9a (E9667); MIc (C5022) 504A (C750), 504J (B3202) 504K (E3450), Pup, Dolphin
7 Training Squadron	Founded on 14 March 1919 by re-designating 3 Fighting School	Disbanded in October 1919 at Sedgeford	Aircraft not known

Glossary

Ace	A pilot who had shot down at least 5 enemy aircraft
Allies	Those forces who were fighting against the Germans
BE2a/c	British reconnaissance and light bomber aircraft
BEF	British Expeditionary Force
CFC	Central Flying School
DFC	Distinguished Flying Cross
DH4	two-seat British bomber
DH5	Single-seat British fighter plane
DH9A	two-seat British bomber
DSC	Distinguished Service Cross
DSO	Distinguished Service Order
FE2a/b	British reconnaissance and fighter aircraft
Flight	Formation of RFC aircraft, usually commanded by a captain
Gotha	German Bomber
MC	Military Cross
MM	Military Medal
OOC	Out of Control
RAF	Royal Air Force
RFC	Royal Flying Corps
RNAS	Royal Naval Air Service
Scout	Fighter aircraft
SE5a	Single-seat British fighter plane
Squadron	Formation of RFC flights, usually commanded by a major
Wing	Group of RFC (RAF) squadrons
WW I	World War One
WW II	World War Two
VC	Victoria Cross
Zeppelin	German Airship

References

Action Stations Revisited Volume No 1 Eastern England by Michael JF Bowyer

Flying Units of the RAF by Alan Lake

Fighter Squadrons of the RAF and Their Aircraft by John Rawlings

Sampson Low Guide World Aircraft, Origins – World War 1

Death from the Skies - The Zeppelin Raids over Norfolk by R.J. Wyatt

Various articles from the *Cross & Cockade International Journals*

Into the Blue by Wing Commander Norman Macmillan OBE MC AFC

The Royal Flying Corps by Terry C. Treadwell and Alan C. Wood

The RFC/RNAS Handbook 1914-18 by Peter G. Cooksley

The Source Book of the RAF by Ken Delve

The Fighters – The Men and Machines of the First Air War by Thomas R. Funderburk

SE5/5a Aces of World War 1 by Norman Franks

Strategy and Intelligence: British Policy during the First World War by Michael L Dockrill and David French

The First Air War – A Pictorial History 1914-1919 by Terry C. Treadwell and Alan C. Wood

Frankfurt – By Night and Day, two accounts of long distance bombing by Peter Chapman.

An Airman Marches by Harold Balfour

Pioneer Pilot by William Armstrong

Mountbatten the official biography by Philip Ziegler

Various aviation internet sites too numerous to mention individually

Mountbatten the official biography by Philip Ziegler

David Jacklin
2 Fairways
Stuston
Diss
Norfolk IP21 4AB

Tel: 01379 741884
e-mail: djacklin@aol.com

16 August 2008

Dear Mr Ross,

Please find your copy of the book *Whin Close Warriors – The story of Sedgeford Aerodrome and its Flying Units.*

I have enclosed an order form, in case you know of others who would wish to order a copy of this or other books.

Best wishes,

David Jacklin

Norfolk Aviation Books by David Jacklin

www.davidjacklin.co.uk

'Up in all Weather' - The Story of RAF Docking £7.50 (£5.00)

RAF Docking began life as a decoy site and emergency landing ground for nearby Bircham Newton, but it soon expanded and took on a life of its own as a base for meteorological reconnaissance, air-sea rescue and offensive operations at night.

The history of this forgotten airfield is vividly told by an ex-RAF Squadron Leader who, as a child just after the war, lived in one of the huts on the site. Aspects of wartime Docking are woven into the tale, as are the memories of men and women who served there. This book will appeal equally to aviation enthusiasts and to local readers who remember or are curious about the dark days of World War II.

'Whin Close Warriors' – The Story of Sedgeford Aerodrome £5.00 (£4.00)

Sedgeford aerodrome opened in 1915 as a night or emergency landing ground for the Royal Naval Air Service station at Great Yarmouth. The RNAS station was employed on home defence duties, responsible for intercepting and destroying Zeppelin airships that were bombing east coast targets at that time. It was later used for the same purpose by Royal Flying Corps and Royal Air Force units, when they assumed responsibility for home defence.

From early 1916 until its closure, Sedgeford was also extensively used to train units that were being deployed to the Western Front and other theatres of war. Fledgling squadrons would undergo several months of intensive flying training and gunnery practice at Sedgeford to prepare them for combat. Flying was in its infancy and the training was rudimentary by today's standards. Inevitably accidents occurred and lives were lost during these frenetic preparations for war. Aspects of the home defence against Zeppelin airships and the training of young airmen are woven into the story, as are the wartime exploits of the Sedgeford-trained units deployed overseas. This book will appeal to aviation enthusiasts and to local readers who are interested in their heritage or in the history of the Great War.

'The Super Handley' - The Story of Britain's First V-Bomber £5.00 (£4.00)

The Handley Page V/1500 was the largest British plane of the First World War and arguably the first real strategic bomber, being specifically designed to attack Berlin from bases in eastern England. Although the Armistice was signed before the V/1500 was used in anger, and it saw only limited post-war service with the Royal Air Force at Bircham Newton, it was to be involved in some notable overseas adventures. These included a through flight from England to India, a successful bombing mission over Kabul and an unfortunate odyssey in North America.

The V/1500 was the forerunner of the Lancaster and other large bombers, which carried the battle to the heart of Nazi Germany throughout World War 2, and an ancestor of the V-bombers used to provide the nuclear deterrent throughout most of the Cold War. The V/1500, the original 'Berlin Bomber', has a special place in British aviation history. This account will appeal to those who are interested in the Great War or the history of aviation.

'From Kipper Kites to Kestrels' – RAF Bircham Newton

£5.00 (£4.00)

This informative book charts the history of Bircham Newton and its satellites, providing details of the origins in World War One, Coastal Command operations during WW2, and administrative training in the post-war period. Details of flying units and their aircraft are also provided.

e-books: As an alternative, all of the above books are available as e-books (in pdf format), readable on your computer using Adobe Reader. These are supplied on CDs at the reduced prices shown in brackets.

If you wish to order any of these books or CDs, please use the order form provided below:

Order Form

To: David Jacklin, 2 Fairways, Stuston, Diss, Norfolk IP21 4AB
Tel: 01379 741884
e-mail: djacklin@aol.com

Please send .... copy/copies of ....

Please add £1:00 postage and packing per book, or 50p per CD.

I enclose a cheque made payable to David Jacklin for £ ....

PLEASE SUPPLY YOUR DETAILS BELOW IN BLOCK CAPITALS

Name ....

Address ....

....

....Post Code.......................

Tel No ....

Please note that two prices are shown against each book. The first price is for a conventional paper book, while the bracketed price is for an e-book, supplied on a CD. Multiple books could be supplied on a single CD, to save postage costs.

FOR MULTIPLE ORDERS, PLEASE USE THE SPACE BELOW:

About the Author

David Jacklin, who grew up in the Norfolk village of Docking, is a military aviation enthusiast and trustee of the RAF Bircham Newton Memorial Project, established to conserve the history of RAF Bircham Newton and its WW2 satellite airfields. Bircham Newton was a close neighbour and sister aerodrome to Sedgeford from 1918 until 1920.

David is a former Royal Air Force Squadron Leader and Systems Engineer who was employed by the Supreme Headquarters Allied Powers Europe (SHAPE) in Belgium. He is now retired, living near Diss on the Norfolk/ Suffolk border. His previous book, '*Up in all Weather' – The Story of RAF Docking*, was published by the Larks Press in 2004.

David can be reached on the telephone at 01379 741884 or by e-mail at djacklin@aol.com.

He can also be contacted via his website at www.davidjacklin.co.uk or via the RAF Bircham Newton project website www.rafbnmp.org.uk